Quizmas

PENGUIN CANADA

QUIZMAS

GORDON PAPE is the author of many
acclaimed books, including bestselling
investment guides, novels,
and non-fiction humour.
He is the father of three and
grandfather of seven, and has
spent many Christmases playing
Quizmas with friends and family.
DEBORAH KERBEL, Gordon's
daughter, is a seasoned *Quizmas* player and mother
of a young son. She is the author of Kendra's
Chronicles, a series of four children's novels. Gordon
and his family live in the Toronto area.

Quizmas

CHRISTMAS
TRIVIA
FAMILY
FUN

GORDON PAPE

WITH
DEBORAH KERBEL

PENGUIN
CANADA

PENGUIN CANADA

Published by the Penguin Group

Penguin Group (Canada), 90 Eglinton Avenue East, Suite 700, Toronto, Ontario, Canada M4P 2Y3
(a division of Pearson Penguin Canada Inc.)

Penguin Group (USA) Inc., 375 Hudson Street, New York, New York 10014, U.S.A.
Penguin Books Ltd, 80 Strand, London WC2R 0RL, England
Penguin Ireland, 25 St Stephen's Green, Dublin 2, Ireland (a division of Penguin Books Ltd)
Penguin Group (Australia), 250 Camberwell Road, Camberwell, Victoria 3124, Australia
(a division of Pearson Australia Group Pty Ltd)
Penguin Books India Pvt Ltd, 11 Community Centre, Panchsheel Park, New Delhi – 110 017, India
Penguin Group (NZ), cnr Airborne and Rosedale Roads, Albany, Auckland 1310, New Zealand
(a division of Pearson New Zealand Ltd)
Penguin Books (South Africa) (Pty) Ltd, 24 Sturdee Avenue, Rosebank, Johannesburg 2196, South Africa

Penguin Books Ltd, Registered Offices: 80 Strand, London WC2R 0RL, England

First published 2004

3 4 5 6 7 8 9 10 (KR)

LIBRARY AND ARCHIVES CANADA CATALOGUING IN PUBLICATION

Pape, Gordon, 1936–
Quizmas : Christmas family trivia fun / Gordon Pape with Deborah Kerbel.

Includes bibliographical references.
ISBN 0-14-301616-4

1. Christmas—Miscellanea. I. Kerbel, Deborah II. Title.

GT4985.P36 2004   394.2663   C2004-904578-4

Visit the Penguin Group (Canada) website at **www.penguin.ca**

Visit the *Quizmas* website at **www.quizmas.net**

To children everywhere
May the magic of Christmas be a part of your life always

Contents

acknowledgments

M any people have contributed question ideas to this book. In fact, whenever I mentioned that I was working on it, someone in the room inevitably came up with a few suggestions, many of which I have used. My thanks to you all, and my apologies if I forget to mention anyone.

My biggest debt of gratitude goes to my daughter, Deborah Kerbel, who is an integral part of our own family holiday traditions. She came up with the original idea of Quizmas and spent many, many hours researching books and surfing the internet to find a wide range of questions. At least a quarter of this book is a direct result of her efforts.

Also thanks to my daughter-in-law, Christine (Katya) Schmied, who thought up many of the questions you will see in the chapters titled Christmas Present, Olde Tyme Christmas, and The Nativity Story.

Others who provided ideas for this book include Diane McCabe, Jane Bradley, Jordan Sullivan, Dan Brintnell, the late David Tafler, Kendra Pape-Green, Kimberley Pape-Green, the late Robert Nelles, Ted Turner, Mike Daigneault, Mike Woolgar, and Ed Mannion. My thanks to you all.

Special thanks to the team at Penguin Canada for their enthusiastic support of this project. I owe a special debt of gratitude to my editors, Andrea Crozier and Judy Phillips, and to Catherine Dorton, who guided us through the whole production process.

Also, thank you to the many authors who have written in-depth books on the origins and history of Christmas and to those who have created the countless internet sites that deal with the subject. You will find a list of source references in the Bibliography.

introduction

I 've always loved the Christmas season, but when I was a child, Christmas was very different from the extended holiday season of today. I grew up at a time when there were no shopping malls, no big-box stores, no television sets, no computers, no internet.

As far as I was concerned, the holiday season really began when the mailman deposited the annual Christmas catalogues from Sears Roebuck and Montgomery Ward in our box. I would spend the next several days poring over them, telling my parents in no uncertain terms exactly what I wanted.

Actual Christmas shopping consisted of little more than a trip to the gift shop attached to Pitkin's, the Rexall Drugstore in nearby Whitehall, Michigan, that exists to this day. The rest of the gifts came in the mail, as far as I know. Apparently the packages all arrived while I was in school, so I was never aware that Santa was really the U.S. Post Office.

It was the 1940s, a time when the whole world lived under the shadow of war. I was five years old when Pearl Harbor was bombed. I have no recollection of the event, but I do remember the impact that the Second World War had on our Christmases for years after.

The greatest loss was the people. Chris, the oldest brother of my best friend, Fred Weber, was no longer part of their family Christmas

Eve celebrations, to which I was often invited when I was older. Instead, he was off fighting on a foreign battlefield.

Sherman and Marshall, both sons of the Lloyd family that lived just down the road and who were always very kind to me, were also in the armed services. Marshall was a flight engineer on a B-24 Liberator bomber and later became an instructor, stationed at an army Air Corps base in Kansas. Sherman was a radio officer and a top turret gunner on a B-24 and saw action in North Africa, Italy, and over the German-held Romanian oil refineries. He always had an artistic bent and, after the war ended, he went with a United Service Organizations (USO) group to Japan, where he entertained the troops and studied the history of Japanese theatre. He brought back several examples of Japanese art, which he would tell me stories about.

I missed them all while they were away, because they were the older brothers I never actually had. Thankfully, they all came home safely. In fact, Marshall, who died in early 2004, lived with his wife, Mary, in the house they built after the war on the lot next to ours. His son John now occupies a home that he and his wife, Barbara, built on the site of the house where I grew up.

During the war years, rationing took its toll on the festivities. It meant that we couldn't always get the sugar my mother needed to bake those special Christmas chocolate chip cookies I loved so much. Meat was scarce and gasoline rationing limited our trips into town. Signs appeared on family-run stores that we once frequented: "Closed for the duration." At the time, I never fully understood what "the duration" meant.

Of course, I was much too young for military service. But my parents dressed me in a soldier suit for one family Christmas portrait perhaps their small tribute to the men fighting and dying overseas. I still have the picture.

Now that I look back on it, I realize that the Christmas music of the period had a distinctly nostalgic tone: "I'll Be Home for Christmas" (1943), "White Christmas" (1942), "Have Yourself a Merry Little Christmas" (1944). Christmas movies often reflected the war, with *Holiday Inn* a classic example.

But through it all, my parents somehow managed to keep the magic in my Christmases, however bleak the rest of the world might be. As I look back now, I sometimes feel guilty that I should have been so lucky while so many people were suffering. It makes me all the more thankful to have the wonderful memories I do.

During those sombre years, Christmas was kept in perspective. As I recall, radio stations didn't start playing carols until after American Thanksgiving. We only began singing them in school in December.

The most fun I had with a Christmas song in my youth was when Mrs. DeWitt taught our kindergarten class at Montague Township School to sing "Up on the Housetop," complete with motions and sound effects. We all loved snapping our fingers at the "click, click, click" part. And the boys took special delight in shouting out the last word in the line "Also a ball and a whip that CRACKS."

We had an assortment of Christmas records at home, which we listened to on what was at the time a state-of-the-art 78-rpm record player. Today, it's an antique, which I still have in the basement. My mother loved Bing Crosby's "White Christmas," and I remember the record it was on—the black Decca label, the scratchiness from incessant playing, and Bing warbling about this dream of his.

I could never figure out what he was carrying on about. The area of Michigan where we lived was true Christmas country. We were right on the shores of Lake Michigan, smack in the middle of one of the continent's great snow belts. There was never any question of whether we would have a white Christmas. Rather, the concern was whether the plows would be able to get through in time to allow my mother to get the turkey and fixings for the meal and for the milkman to deliver the requisite chocolate milk and eggnog for the event.

When "White Christmas" wasn't playing, Bing would be singing some other holiday song, such as "Christmas in Killarney," "I'll Be Home for Christmas," and "It's Beginning to Look a Lot Like Christmas." At those times, I retreated to my room and read a book.

That all changed one Christmas morning when I was about ten. One of my gifts was a two-record album called *The Nutcracker Suite,* by my favourite musical artist of the day, Spike Jones. I wasn't familiar with the music and didn't learn until years later that *The Nutcracker* was a ballet. What enthralled me were the lyrics and the imaginative story they told. That's right, the lyrics—Spike Jones and his arrangers had written words to the music. Through them, I learned the story of Clara who, one Christmas Eve while sleeping, is transported to the Land of the Sugar Plums. I pictured in my mind the dancing Russian doll, the waltzing flowers, and the prancing tin flute. It all culminated with a titanic battle between the Nutcracker and the Mouse King that ended when Clara threw her shoe at the Mouse King and knocked him down, just when he seemed to be getting the best of our hero. When the Nutcracker then changed into a handsome prince, the world was put right again.

I played that album over and over every Christmas for the rest of my childhood. Even today, almost sixty years later, I can still remember most of the words.

After writing this, I went on a search through our dusty 78-rpm albums, long stored away and forgotten, hoping I could find the album so my grandchildren could enjoy it. Alas, it has gone. But I did come across the old "White Christmas" recording. Mother would have been pleased.

I played that album over and over every Christmas for the rest of my

The ritual that began every holiday season was to go to the attic and bring down the boxes that contained our nativity scene. I still remember the joy of unwrapping the separate pieces from the tissue into which they had been carefully placed the year previous.

The biggest box held a large replica of the stable, which was beautifully handcrafted. This was placed on a white cloth that was spread on the baby grand piano in our living room.

A second box contained detailed, hand-painted figurines of Joseph, Mary, Baby Jesus, the Wise Men, and assorted shepherds, angels, and animals: little lambs, donkeys, goats, and a big cow. We would carefully unwrap each piece, and I would have the honour of placing it in its proper place in the display. Last came the infant Jesus, who my mother always trusted me to place tenderly in his manger.

When it was all set up, my mother would strategically arrange some lights around the scene so that it became the focal point of the room—at least until the Christmas tree went up a week or so later.

Another ritual was listening to the special Christmas radio programs. I would never miss my favourites, even though the same shows were repeated every year. Since we lived far from any major city, I didn't grow up with Santa Claus parades and department store Santas. There was no television, so the radio was my only link to Christmas in other parts of the country.

There were two programs in particular that I never tired of. One was *The Cinnamon Bear,* which was broadcast from Chicago on station WGN. The program always opened with a theme song, which I learned by heart: "I'm the Cinnamon Bear with the shoe button eyes...."

Cinnamon's many Christmastime adventures captured my imagination and I was right there with him on his treasure island or in Santa's sleigh.

Then, from WTMJ in Milwaukee, we'd get *Billie the Brownie from Schusters*. Schusters was a department store where the kids could go to visit Billie and his pals (and persuade their parents to buy more toys), but I didn't realize that at the time. To me, this broadcast was coming straight from Santa's Workshop at the North Pole (where it was set), where Billie and the other brownies were busily building toys for all the good little boys and girls around the world. For several years, the last thing my mother and I did on Christmas Eve before she tucked me in for the night was listen to the season-ending broadcast in which Billie and buddies load Santa's sleigh, hitch up the eight reindeer (Rudolph wasn't one of the reindeer yet), and wave goodbye as the jolly old elf flew off on his annual trek. Then it was putting out the chocolate chip cookies and milk and off to bed to await the wonders of the morning.

⁂

And then The Day. The excitement of rushing downstairs. The presents. The visits. The turkey. The exhaustion. All magical. All long gone.

I still remember some of the wonderful gifts I received as a child. There was the Lionel electric train that my parents set up to circle around the tree. It was pulled by a big black steam engine crafted in exquisite detail. It would probably fetch a small fortune from a collector today, but it is gone, along with the most of the other memorabilia of my youth.

Then there was my first Hardy Boys book, *The Mystery of Cabin Island*. I can still recall the cover, the brothers peering out from the woods at an isolated log cabin in a snowy wilderness. On a cold December day, the view from our living room window looked very similar. That book opened up the Hardy Boys world to me, and from that point on I devoured every book written by Franklin W. Dixon. But when my mother suggested I might also like to read the Nancy Drew books, I snorted. She was a *girl!*

I received my first chemistry set for Christmas and proceeded to stink up my room by concocting hydrogen sulphide (rotten-egg gas). One year I was given a game called Photo-Electric Football, which was the precursor of modern video games. It was rather primitive, involving overlaying offensive and defensive alignments on a screen and then illuminating them, but we played it for hours on end. Today's kids would scoff, but to us it was a marvel of electronic ingenuity.

And then there was the sled. That wonderful, long-wished-for sled with the shiny red runners. I'd asked Santa for it for years, and finally he delivered. Flexible Flyer, that was the name painted on it, and it was a *real* boy's sled. Not a namby-pamby, pull-baby-around sleigh with protective sides; you could do a real belly flop on the Flexible Flyer. Lying on the windward side of Lake Michigan, we always had snow for Christmas, sometimes far too much. But that year, it was the perfect depth for a kid with a new sled. I could hardly wait to get bundled up and head over to Sunset Trail to try it out.

Now, Sunset Trail was (and is) hardly a path for novice sledders. From the top, it descends a steep slope, winding through bushes and trees along the way, and there are plenty of bumps to provide jolts as you swish down. But that was where the big kids went for action, and with Flexible Flyer I was ready to join their ranks. But when I got there, the run was deserted. After all, it *was* Christmas morning. Everyone else was still ripping off gift wrap. I was disappointed—part of the fun would be to show off Flexible Flyer to the neighbourhood kids. But with or without them, we were going down! I climbed to the top of the hill, Flexible Flyer dutifully trailing behind. There was not the smallest hint of trepidation as I prepared for the maiden voyage. Rather, to this day I can recall the exhilaration I felt. I took a running start, leaped onto the sled face down, grabbed the steering handles on both sides, and off we went. The trees flashed by in a blur. I pulled one handle, then the other, to change directions and we accelerated, faster and faster. Still no fear— there was no time for it. My mind was focused on making Flexible Flyer go ever faster as we came out of the next turn. Now we were nearing the bottom of the trail and travelling at top speed. Suddenly, the sled became airborne. We had hit a mogul and Flexible Flyer had launched into space, with me clinging to it for dear life. It seemed as though we were suspended there forever, although it was only moments. Then *whomp!* We were back on the ground and at the bottom of the trail. Flexible Flyer was in great shape. I can't say the same for me. I lay on the sled gasping and groaning, thinking I had been killed. Actually, I only had the wind knocked out of me, but that had never happened before and I was terrified. Fortunately, a neighbour was walking by with her dog and came to my rescue. After a few moments, I was fully recovered and ready for another go. Flexible Flyer and I were pals for years afterward.

Of course, there were also some Christmas disappointments. One year when I was about six years old, a big box arrived in the mail from a friend of my mother who lived in Milwaukee. I knew her as Auntie Edna even though she wasn't actually a relative. We lived on a rural route where the mailman delivered by car. Since the package was too big to leave in the box, he came to the door. I happened to be home from school that day, and when I answered the door, he said something like, "Are you Master Gordon Pape?" When I said yes, he handed me the box with a cheery, "Looks like a Christmas present for you." That's how I found out about it in advance. If my mother had answered the door, she would have hidden the package until Christmas morning.

I begged her to allow me to open it right away, but she was firm. "It says right on the box 'Do Not Open Until Christmas,'" she told me. "Auntie Edna wants it to be a surprise."

I was very excited by the possibilities. It was about ten days before the great event and I didn't know whether I could wait that long. My mother stripped away the brown mailing paper and put the brightly wrapped box under the tree, where it tormented me every time I looked at it. I was sorely tempted to sneak a peek when my mother wasn't looking, but I knew I couldn't do so without her discovering. So I waited, impatiently.

On Christmas morning I dashed down the stairs, took in the array of presents under the tree, and made straight for Auntie Edna's big box. I tore off the wrapping paper, opened the lid, and found—a sweater! A lousy sweater! My mother insisted it was a beautiful, hand-knit sweater, but that didn't impress me one bit. I wanted a game, a microscope, some new trains, a basketball, whatever. Anything but a sweater!

I guess my mother never conveyed my views to Auntie Edna because every year thereafter another box arrived bearing clothes. It was the last present I opened each Christmas Day—I knew what to expect!

I always sent a thank-you letter though. My mother was insistent on that point. I confess now, however, that my heart wasn't in it. Sorry, Auntie Edna. But thanks for the thought.

✦

One of the few Christmas Eve rituals that I did not enjoy as a child was my father's annual reading of *A Christmas Carol*. It was, to put it bluntly, an ordeal that had to be endured before the fun of the following morning.

How, you may wonder, could anyone have such unhappy memories about the world's best-loved Christmas tale? Easily. Just try reading it all the way through to young children and watch what happens. First will come the fidgeting, then the yawning, and finally the kids will fall off to sleep long before the Ghost of Christmas Yet to Come puts in an appearance—if they don't stage an outright rebellion first.

The fact is that Charles Dickens' classic novella is simply not a children's story. The words are too long, the prose is too convoluted, and there are few characters, apart from Tiny Tim, who kids can relate to.

Today, of course, there are many children's versions of the story that are much better suited to short attention spans and limited vocabularies. But when I was a boy, it was all or nothing—and my father determined that it would be all. Perhaps he just did it as a way to get me to fall asleep early. If that was his goal, he certainly succeeded!

I tried reading *A Christmas Carol* to my children only once. Watching their reaction as I did so brought those memories flooding back. I never read it to them again but, rather, let them come to it in their own time.

I did discover another Dickens' Christmas story that was much more to their liking, however. Indeed, for several years they demanded that I read it to them every Christmas Eve.

It was the Christmas at Dingley Dell in "A Good-Humoured Christmas Chapter" from *The Pickwick Papers,* which is full of marvellous, warm depictions of the glorious day in Victorian England, complete with a great feast, music and dancing, parlour games, skating parties, roaring fireplaces, and a wonderfully funny character known only as the "fat boy."

One of the most intriguing parts of the Dingley Dell Christmas is a ghost story told by Mr. Wardle, which my children loved. (Telling ghost stories at Christmastime was a tradition in bygone years.) The title of the chapter is "The Story of the Goblins Who Stole a Sexton," and while it is quite long, my kids would listen all the way through.

The tale revolves around a working-man's version of Scrooge, a mean-hearted gravedigger by the name of Gabriel Grub (Dickens was a master when it came to names). Grub is the kind of unpleasant character who beats small boys for singing Christmas songs too loudly, and who digs graves on Christmas Eve. But this particular Christmas Eve is different when he finds, sitting on a tombstone, a "strange, unearthly figure" that turns out to be a goblin. You can read the rest for yourself. It may sound rather dark for a Christmas Eve tale, but so is *A Christmas Carol* until the very end. And, like Scrooge, Gabriel Grub emerges from his ghostly encounters a much-changed man.

Just a word of warning if you decide to read this to your own youngsters. Go through the chapter first and do a bit of abridging— there is some violence in the Gabriel Grub tale, which you may wish to leave out or moderate. Keep the funny parts, the descriptive scenes of Dingley Dell, and the action. Use your best narrative voice to make the characters come alive, keep the reading to no more than twenty minutes, and I think you may have some success in introducing your young ones to the wonderful Christmas world of Charles Dickens.

Dickensian Christmases, of course, took place in England, and I was fortunate enough to experience the holiday season there first-hand.

Our family moved to England in the summer of 1970. I had been named London Bureau Chief for a national Canadian newspaper chain. It was a coveted posting and a great honour, so although we hated to leave our comfortable home in Ottawa, we packed our bags, loaded ourselves and two young children on a plane, and took off for the grand adventure.

It almost led to a family breakdown.

England is one of our cultural touchstones. I have always loved the literature and history of the country, and both my wife and I asked repeatedly before our departure, "How different can it be?" After all, the English speak the same language, have the same values, eat similar foods, and share a common background.

Thus, we were totally unprepared for the cultural shock, which was compounded when, within two weeks of our arrival, I was assigned to Belfast to cover the escalating violence in Northern Ireland, leaving my wife in London to fend for herself and the children.

Later she told me that she came within a hair of bundling the kids on a plane and going home.

After several months of tribulations, it was Christmastime. But we weren't in a celebratory mood. London didn't look like Christmas, and it didn't feel like Christmas.

Everything was green and foggy and damp. We'd always complained about the snow and cold in Ottawa, but now we were feeling nostalgic for it. Going Christmas shopping in a drizzle was depressing.

The shopping experience itself was even worse. London did its best to look cheery, with bright lights and colourful store windows decorating Oxford Street. But the crowds! The sidewalks were so jammed with people that you had to push your way to get anywhere. The hordes in front of the toy displays made it almost impossible to see anything. Disappointed children wailed, and frustrated adults lost their traditional British stoicism. It was a most unpleasant time.

And then something happened. I won't describe it as miraculous, but it was certainly extraordinary.

On Christmas Eve, it began to snow. Soft, fat, wet flakes came tumbling out of the sky. And they continued throughout the night while the children slept and Santa came and went.

In the morning, the sun came out for the first time in two weeks and shone down on a true winter landscape. The snow clung to the tree branches, crowned the street lamps, and hid London's usual grime beneath a blanket of white.

It also buried the roads, to the consternation of my cousin in Rochester, south of London, who was coming with her family for Christmas dinner. They would have to take the train instead of driving. Inconvenient, but they made it—and agreed that the white Christmas, something they had never seen before, was quite magical.

The snow began to melt on Boxing Day. By New Year's Day, all trace of it was gone. But after that, our life in England started to improve. The white Christmas was the turning point.

Later I read in *Christmas Watching,* a wonderful little book by British author Desmond Morris, that London experienced only two white Christmases in the twentieth century: in 1938, and our own 1970 White Christmas.

It made me realize how truly special that day was.

We all have Christmas traditions in our lives. Many of them have been handed down to us by our cultures and religions, others are modern, still others are the product of our family dynamics.

In our home, for example, it has always been a tradition to eat a meal of *tourtière* on Christmas Eve. These spicy pork pies are a mainstay on Quebec tables at Christmastime, and my wife, being half French-Canadian, has made them a part of our holiday celebrations, wherever in the world we happen to be.

Sometimes, however, attempts to start new family Christmas traditions fail miserably. Let me tell you about one such incident.

It happened when our three children were very young. I decided that rather than go to the garden centre to buy a Christmas tree, we would venture into the forest and cut our own, just like in the good old days. There were ads in the paper for Christmas-tree farms that allowed this, so one Saturday in mid-December I bundled the kids into the car and off we went.

It was a grey day, with a sky that looked like it might send a few snowflakes swirling down to add a festive touch to our hunt. Unfortunately, by the time we found our way to the tree farm, what was falling was not flakes but drizzle. The dirt road leading to the farm was a sea of mud and packed with cars. I began to get a bad feeling about the whole adventure.

The kids were gung-ho, however. My son had brought a little axe along and raced off ahead, prepared to start chopping at the first sign of a tree. But the hillside where the farm was located looked like a bomb had been dropped on it. There wasn't a tree to be seen—only hundreds of small stumps.

"Down in the valley," said the lady in charge as she warmed her hands over an oil-barrel fire. She gestured with her thumb. "Should be a few left there somewhere."

We trudged down the barren hill. The drizzle had turned to rain and the wind was up. I thought the day couldn't get much worse when my youngest daughter, who was five at the time, piped up, "I have to go to the bathroom!" Of course, there was no bathroom for miles around. Tree farms don't come with mod cons, and those were the days before portable potties.

"Just wait," I urged. "We won't be long." Being that there still wasn't a tree in sight, it was wishful thinking.

A few minutes later, my older daughter joined in the whining. "I'm cold. I'm tired." I sympathized; I was too. I was about to abandon the hunt when my son shouted, "There's one!" and dashed off. We followed through the gloom and found him hacking away at the most scrawny tree you could imagine. The only reason it was still standing was that no one else wanted it. But at that point, we didn't have much choice, especially after another, louder, wail of "I have to go to the bathroom!" He chopped. The tree came down. I dragged it back, paid the barrel lady $5, and herded the soggy children into the car. The first stop was a gas station for my daughter to find relief. The next stop was home.

"We got one, we got one," my son shouted, running to the door to tell his mother. "I cut it down myself." She smiled benignly—until she saw the puny tree. Then her face turned as dark as the sky. "Not in my house," she proclaimed firmly.

We compromised by erecting the miserable pine in the entry way, where my son could proudly show it to visitors. The next day we went to the garden centre and bought a proper tree for the living room.

We never went to a tree farm again. Some traditions just aren't meant to be.

Today, my greatest Christmas pleasure is sharing the day with my grandchildren and watching their faces reflect the wonder and excitement that I felt as a boy. I only hope they are experiencing the intensity of pleasure that I did at this most special time of all, although I sometimes think that we have made Christmas too overwhelming for them. Every year my wife and I resolve to cut back a bit on the gifts. And every year we arrive at our children's doorstep carrying bags and boxes filled with presents. We can't help it. The world has more than its share of troubles these days. Let one day be set aside for peace, happiness, and, for our children and grandchildren, magic.

sHare your cHristmas memories

We all have special memories of Christmas. I've included some of mine in this book and I hope you've enjoyed reading about them.

Perhaps you have your own Christmas memory or tradition that you would like to share, something that you think would bring joy or fun or hope or faith to others. It can be anything from a favourite Christmas recipe to the recollection of a life-changing Christmas event. If so, we would love to hear from you. We'll post as many as we can on our website, and perhaps we can put together a book of Christmas nostalgia that people around the world can enjoy.

If your submission is selected for book publication, we'll send you a cheque for $100 that you can put toward your Christmas shopping.

To participate, write down your favourite Christmas memory and mail it to me c/o "Christmas Memories" at the address you'll find at the back of this book, on page 203, or go to our website at www.quizmas.net and use the Christmas Memory email form there. Please try to keep your submissions under 1,000 words.

Don't be shy. Christmas is about giving, and one of the most valuable things we can give to anyone are good memories, because when we're gone, so are they.

PLaying Quizmas

We all think we know everything there is to know about Christmas. And why not? It's been a part of our lives for as long as we can remember. Like many of you, from the time I was a small child I have heard the story of the birth of Baby Jesus, sung carols in Sunday school, hung up my stocking on Christmas Eve, and eagerly awaited the arrival of Santa Claus.

As we grew older, we each discovered new dimensions to the Christmas season. Some of us adapted traditional foods and customs from the countries of our parents or grandparents or more distant ancestors. We read classic tales such as *A Christmas Carol* and tried to apply their messages to our own lives. We went to Christmas movies, listened to Christmas songs on the radio, watched Christmas specials on TV, stayed in touch with friends and loved ones by writing Christmas cards, shopped for that special Christmas gift, revelled in the traditional Christmas dinner.

So we should know just about everything there is to know about Christmas, shouldn't we? Well, you may be surprised at just how much you and your family *don't* know.

Over the years, I've collected all kinds of Christmas-related trivia. Some comes from my own memories, some from the experiences of others, some from the Bible, some from the stories of Charles Dickens, some from other books, some from newspaper articles—whenever I see a new story or fact about Christmas, I cut it out—and some from more modern sources, such as the internet.

A few years ago, my daughter Deborah suggested that I use some of this trivia to create a game. It sounded like it might be fun, so I put together a Christmas quiz for the family, which I called Quizmas. Everyone got a kick out of it, despite some complaints that my questions were too tough. But even when they were stumped, they were eager to learn the right answer. Okay, in what sport *do* teams compete for the Santa Claus Cup, granddad?

Since my family had fun with these trivia questions, I thought that others would too, hence this book. *Quizmas* was written with the wish that it might add just a little more fun to the Christmas festivities, for both children and their parents and grandparents.

Some of the questions in this book may leave you muttering, "I know that, I know that, just give me a second." For example, almost everyone who has seen the classic movie *It's a Wonderful Life* can come up with the name of Jimmy Stewart as the lead actor without a moment's hesitation. But what is the name of the character he plays? And what town does he live in? If you haven't seen the movie lately, you may find yourself scratching your head in frustration!

Many people have incorporated centuries-old traditions into their Christmas rituals without having the least idea where they come from. We kiss under the mistletoe, but do you know why? Are the lights on the Christmas tree just pretty decorations or do they have some deeper symbolism? And speaking of Christmas trees, where did that idea come from? Why would we bring a fir tree into our homes, hang ornaments on it, and treat it as the focal point of Christmas morning?

What do you really know about the carols that we joyfully sing every Christmas season? Are you aware that Good King Wenceslas was a real person? Did you know that the words to "O Holy Night" were written by a wine merchant? Your children sing "Away in a Manger," but do they know what a manger is?

In many cases, you may not know the answers to the questions you'll find here, but I think you'll be intrigued by them. Did you know, for instance, that Christmas was abolished for a time in both the United States and England? Do your children know they can track Santa's progress on Christmas Eve on the internet? Have you heard that a major war was stopped to celebrate Christmas and that soldiers from both sides exchanged gifts on the battlefield?

In the course of our research, we found that there is not universal agreement about some issues. We discovered that a few so-called traditions are actually only modern urban legends. We found differing views on the origins of some of our Christmas rituals and, not surprisingly, on the details of the nativity story itself, beyond what is written in the Gospels of St. Matthew and St. Luke (which in turn contradict each other on some details). So in some cases you may find that the answer we give to a question is at odds with what you have read or heard elsewhere. That should come as no surprise, being that much of the history of Christmas is shrouded by the mists of centuries. Where we have encountered conflicting views, we have selected an answer that corresponds to the general consensus on the subject, as far as we can ascertain it. But if there is a valid disagreement about one of our answers, don't argue about it. Be generous and give the benefit of a doubt. It's Christmas, after all!

How to Play the Game

Everyone can play Quizmas— there are questions in each chapter for both kids (Tots to Teens) and grown-ups (although sometimes the grown-ups get stumped by the kids' questions!). The questions have been divided into categories, each with its own chapter, and all, except the bonuses, are multiple choice. Each question has a difficulty rating from one to three. Correct answers receive points equal to the weighting. Some questions have more than one correct answer, but be careful! Grown-ups who get one of them wrong may be penalized. (After all, they're supposed to know more about Christmas than the kids.)

The children's questions are divided into three groups:

Sugar Plums

These are the easiest questions and each has a point value of one. They're the best choices for the children under six in the family.

Candy Canes

This set of questions is a little harder (just like candy canes are) and are worth two points each. They're best suited for children in the age range of six to nine.

Peanut Brittle

These are the toughies, and the three points they earn reflect that. Reserve them for the older children in the game.

In the same way, there are three categories of questions for grown-ups:

Pumpkin Pies

For anyone with any knowledge of Christmas, these should be as easy as the traditional dessert they are named after. One point each.

Plum Puddings

The questions get more complex in this category and you may come across some surprises, just as you might in the old-fashioned English plum pudding. Two points each.

Chestnuts

These will be the toughest nuts to crack, which is why they're worth three points if you get the right answer.

Bonus Questions

Some questions have bonuses. If the original question is answered correctly, the player may attempt the bonus and receive extra points (as many as the question was worth) if it is answered correctly as well.

The game can be enjoyed in many ways. Here are some suggestions.

Family Quizmas

A few days before Christmas, select twenty questions for grown-ups and twenty for children. Try to make both sets approximately equal in weight. Type up question sheets and print them. On Christmas Day, pass out copies and give everyone fifteen minutes to choose answers. Then tally the scores. Have small prizes ready for the winners.

Social Quizmas

Have one person select questions from the book at random. If children are playing, alternate between the grown-ups' and children's questions. Read each question aloud and let everyone guess and

discuss the answer. You'll be surprised at how many grown-ups' questions the kids get right.

team Quizmas

Divide players into teams of four. Give each team a piece of paper and a pencil. Read out the questions and allow thirty seconds for the teams to confer and write down their answers. Top score at the end wins.

Generations Quizmas

Have grown-ups form one team, children the other. Read out questions from each category alternatively. Each team answers only its own group's questions and has thirty seconds to do so. Top score wins a prize.

Category Quizmas

This can be used as a variation of any of the games. Select only one category for the competition. Alternatively, in a team game, each team can select the category from which the question is to be asked.

Party Quizmas

Having friends over for a Christmas party? Select twenty questions, then type up a question sheet and make copies. Give one to each person upon arrival. Announce that at a specific time you'll collect the sheets and tally the results, with a prize going to the winner. This is a great conversation-starter.

So now open the book to a topic of interest and choose some questions to get started. Everyone will have fun, and maybe you'll learn something new and interesting about a holiday that means so much to so many of us. Enjoy.

Santa and friends

tots to teens puzzlers

Sugar Plums

1. Which of these is not one of Santa's original reindeer?
   a. Cupid   b. Rudolph   c. Dancer   d. Comet

2. Which of these is not another name for Santa Claus?
   a. Kris Kringle   c. Father Christmas
   b. St. Nicholas   d. Jack Frost

3. Who makes all of Santa's toys in his workshop?
   a. Gnomes   b. Elves   c. Dwarves   d. Fairies

4. Including Rudolph, how many reindeer does Santa have?
   a. Six   b. Seven   c. Nine   d. Twelve

5. What is the traditional snack to leave out for Santa on Christmas Eve?
   a. Wine and cheese   c. Cocoa and cake
   b. Coffee and donuts   d. Milk and cookies

6. What does Santa Claus wear on his feet while delivering presents around the world?
   a. Sandals   b. Slippers   c. Boots   d. Galoshes

7. What does Santa Claus carry all his toys in?

    a. A briefcase   b. A tote bag   c. A magic sack   d. A shopping cart

8. In the poem "A Visit from St. Nicholas" (also known as "The Night Before Christmas"), what is Santa's nose described as looking like?

    a. A cherry   b. A raspberry   c. A strawberry   d. A grape

9. What sound does Santa Claus make when he laughs?

    a. Ha Ha Ha   b. Hee Hee Hee   c. Ho Ho Ho   d. Yuk Yuk Yuk

10. What colour is Santa's beard?

    a. Grey   b. White   c. Red   d. Black

11. Which word does *not* describe Santa Claus?

    a. Jolly   b. Generous   c. Merry   d. Grouchy

12. How many times does Santa check his list?

    a. Once   b. Twice   c. Thrice   d. Never

Candy Canes

13. In the poem "A Visit from St. Nicholas," what are Santa's clothes tarnished with?

    a. Ashes and soot   c. Dust and grime

    b. Dirt and mud   d. Cookie crumbs

14. In Australia, Santa's sleigh is often shown as being pulled by which animals?
    a. Koala bears   b. Kangaroos   c. Camels   d. Mule deer

15. According to tradition, what does Santa Claus smoke?
    a. A pipe
    b. A cigar
    c. Cigarettes
    d. Nothing—he knows smoking is bad for you

16. What cuddly character was introduced by Marshall Field's department store as Santa's goodwill ambassador?
    a. Uncle Mistletoe   c. Brother Noël
    b. Grandfather Frost   d. Papa Present

17. Whose float traditionally brings up the rear of New York City's Thanksgiving Day parade?
    a. Spider-Man   c. Santa Claus
    b. Tom Turkey   d. Rudolph the Red-Nosed Reindeer

18. In the poem "A Visit from St. Nicholas," what are Santa's cheeks compared to?
    a. Apples   b. Tomatoes   c. Roses   d. Marshmallows

19. How is Santa sometimes seen arriving in Hawaii?
    a. By helicopter   c. Riding a whale
    b. On a surfboard   d. Driving a dune buggy

20. What is Santa Claus called in England?
    a. St. Nicholas
    b. Father Christmas
    c. Uncle Nick
    d. Big Red

21. What is Santa Claus called in France?
    a. St. Wenceslas
    b. St. Nicholas
    c. Oncle Nicholas
    d. Père Noël

22. Which of these supernatural acts does Santa Claus *not* perform?
    a. Pulling toys from a magic sack
    b. Flying through the air on a sleigh
    c. Travelling around the world in one night
    d. Lifting a white rabbit out of a hat

23. What is the most popular treat for Santa's reindeer at Christmastime?
    a. Carrots   b. Hamburgers   c. Ice cream   d. Soup

24. In Finland, what does Santa Claus always ask before entering a home at Christmas?
    a. Where's the bathroom?
    b. Are there any good children here?
    c. What's for dinner?
    d. Where can I park my sleigh?

Peanut Brittle

25. Which organization tracks the progress of Santa Claus every Christmas Eve?
    a. NATO   b. NORAD   c. NAFTA   d. UNICEF

26. According to the 2001 Annual General Growth Properties Santa Survey, what is Santa Claus's favourite kind of cookie?
    a. Ginger snap   b. Oatmeal   c. Peanut butter   d. Chocolate chip

27. Santa lives at the North Pole. What country is it in?
    a. Norway   b. Canada   c. Russia   d. Greenland

28. According to tradition, how do Santa's reindeer fly?
    a. By flapping very large wings   c. By eating magic corn
    b. By holding their breath   d. By earning a pilot's licence

29. In which country is Santa Claus known as "Santa *no ojisan*" or "Uncle Santa"?
    a. The Philippines   c. Japan
    b. New Zealand   d. Indonesia

30. Which of these things does Santa Claus *not* know about little children?
    a. Their names   c. If they've been bad or good
    b. When they're sleeping   d. Their I.Q. scores

Grown-ups' Brainteasers

Pumpkin Pies

31. Which of these products has the Santa Claus image been used to sell?
    - a. Soap
    - b. Whisky
    - c. Scotch tape
    - d. All three

32. Who popularized the song "Santa Baby"?
    - a. Peggy Lee
    - b. Ella Fitzgerald
    - c. Eartha Kitt
    - d. Doris Day

33. Although he's never been charged, Santa Claus is technically guilty of committing which crime every Christmas?
    - a. Jaywalking
    - b. Trespassing
    - c. Theft
    - d. Obstruction of justice

34. Which European settlers are credited with bringing the concept of Santa Claus to North America?
    - a. English
    - b. French
    - c. Spanish
    - d. Dutch

35. According to the 2001 Annual General Growth Properties Santa Survey, what is the average weight of a shopping mall Santa?
    - a. 118 pounds
    - b. 218 pounds
    - c. 318 pounds
    - d. 418 pounds

36. In the poem "A Visit from St. Nicholas," how many times is Santa Claus's name mentioned?
    a. Zero   b. Five   c. Fifteen   d. Twenty-five

37. Which of these groups of people is St. Nicholas not a patron saint of?
    a. Children   b. Mariners   c. Pawnbrokers   d. Glass-blowers

Plum Puddings

38. St. Nicholas, the inspiration for the modern Santa Claus, lived in what is now which country?
    a. Israel   c. The Netherlands
    b. Italy   d. Turkey

39. In what modern city was the first American church dedicated to St. Nicholas established?
    a. Boston   b. New York   c. Philadelphia   d. Charleston

40. Who is the Russian equivalent of Santa Claus?
    a. Ice Ivan   c. Mother Snow
    b. Grandfather Frost   d. Czar Nicholas

41. What company is widely credited with popularizing the modern image of Santa Claus?
    a. Pepsi-Cola   b. Hershey   c. Coca-Cola   d. Nestlé

42. In what modern country is the original St. Nicholas buried?
    a. Italy   b. Turkey   c. Greece   d. Syria

43. When is the Feast Day of St. Nicholas?
    a. December 24   c. December 6
    b. January 6   d. July 21

44. In eighteenth- and nineteenth-century Europe, what was the Father Christmas figure sometimes shown wearing on his head?
    a. A top hat
    c. A nightcap
    b. A crown of wine glasses and bottles
    d. All three

45. The use of the colours red and white for Santa's clothes became commonplace only in the twentieth century. Why were they chosen?
    a. They are easy to see
    b. They are the colours of the Coca-Cola trademark
    c. They signify the blood and body of Christ
    d. They are the world's most popular colours

46. A legend from which country is believed to have provided the inspiration for the reindeer that draw Santa's sleigh?
    a. Scotland   b. Norway   c. Canada   d. Finland

47. What is the average life expectancy of a real-life reindeer?
    a. Eight years
    c. Twenty-eight years
    b. Eighteen years
    d. Thirty-eight years

Chestnuts

48. Which artist is credited with creating the modern image of Santa Claus?
    a. James McNeill Whistler
    c. John Constable
    b. Thomas Nast
    d. Grandma Moses

49. What is the modern name of the town in which the original St. Nicholas was born?
    a. Haifa   b. Odessa   c. Ankara   d. Petara

50. Which city is widely credited with having the first department store Santa Claus?
    a. London   b. New York   c. Philadelphia   d. Montreal

51. In which U.S. state is the town of Santa Claus located?
    a. Michigan   b. Missouri   c. Indiana   d. Ohio

52. In what year did the historical St. Nicholas die?
    a. 522 A.D.   b. 220 A.D.   c. 1210 A.D.   d. 345 A.D.

53. Santa was burnt in effigy in the 1950s by clergy in what country?
    a. France   b. Italy   c. Honduras   d. Spain

54. What type of hat did Father Christmas wear in England in the nineteenth century?
   a. Top hat   b. Beaver hat   c. Bowler hat   d. Hunter's cap

55. Which classic American writer first described St. Nicholas as a jolly man with a long pipe?
   a. James Fenimore Cooper   c. Washington Irving
   b. Henry Wadsworth Longfellow   d. Henry James

56. At Macy's department store in New York City, what is the average length of time a child sits in Santa's lap?
   a. Seven seconds   c. One minute, seven seconds
   b. Thirty-seven seconds   d. Seven minutes

57. In Austria, which devilish figure accompanies St. Nicholas, carrying a whip?
   a. Beelzebub   b. Krampus   c. Malevol   d. Darth Vader

58. The tradition of placing gifts in stockings is said to have come from gifts given by the original St. Nicholas to three sisters. What were those gifts?
   a. Shoes and stockings to permit them to go on a pilgrimage
   b. Bags of gold to enable them to marry
   c. Clothes for their newborn babies
   d. Food during a time of famine

59. What was the middle name of the author of the poem "A Visit from St. Nicholas"?

    a. Clark   b. Calvin   c. Clement   d. Cuthbert

60. What was the name of the first movie to feature Santa Claus?

    a. *A Fantasy Actually Filmed in Northern Alaska*

    b. *You Better Watch Out*

    c. *The Origins of St. Nicholas*

    d. *The True Tale of Flying Reindeer*

61. Which artist created a new look for Santa that the Coca-Cola company featured in its advertising for many years?

    a. Haddon Sundblom   c. Andy Warhol

    b. Norman Rockwell   d. Walt Disney

62. How did St. Nicholas save a ship that was in peril on the sea?

    a. He calmed the waters

    b. He asked all the passengers to pray

    c. He took over the helm and steered it to safety

    d. He told the crew to throw the entire cargo of wine urns overboard

63. The first depiction of a modern-looking Santa Claus appeared in which magazine?

    a. *Harper's Weekly*   c. *Punch*

    b. *Vanity Fair*   d. *The Illustrated London News*

answers

tots to teens puzzlers

Sugar Plums (1 point each)

1.	b	Rudolph
2.	d	Jack Frost
3.	b	Elves
4.	c	Nine
5.	d	Milk and cookies
6.	c	Boots
7.	c	A magic sack
8	a	A cherry
9.	c	Ho Ho Ho
10.	b	White
11.	d	Grouchy
12.	b	Twice

CaNÒy CaNes (2 poiNts eacH)

13.	a	Ashes and soot
14.	b	Kangaroos
15.	a	A pipe
16.	a	Uncle Mistletoe
17.	c	Santa Claus
18.	a	Apples
19.	b	On a surfboard
20.	b	Father Christmas
21.	d	Père Noël
22.	d	Lifting a white rabbit out of a hat
23.	a	Carrots
24.	b	Are there any good children here?

PeaNut BrittLe (3 poiNts eacH)

25.	b	NORAD (North American Aerospace Defence Command)
26.	d	Chocolate chip
27.	b	Canada
28.	c	By eating magic corn
29.	c	Japan
30.	d	Their I.Q. scores

Grown-ups' Brainteasers

Pumpkin Pies (1 point each)

31.	d	All three
32.	c	Eartha Kitt
33.	b	Trespassing
34.	d	Dutch
35.	b	218 pounds
36.	a	Zero
37.	d	Glass-blowers

Plum Puddings (2 points each)

38.	d	Turkey
39.	b	New York
40.	b	Grandfather Frost
41.	c	Coca-Cola
42.	a	Italy
43.	c	December 6
44.	d	All three
45.	b	They are the colours of the Coca-Cola trademark
46.	d	Finland
47.	a	Eight years

Chestnuts (3 points each)

48.	b	Thomas Nast
49.	d	Petara
50.	c	Philadelphia
51.	c	Indiana
52.	d	345 A.D.
53.	a	France
54.	b	Beaver hat
55.	c	Washington Irving
56.	b	Thirty-seven seconds
57.	b	Krampus
58.	b	Bags of gold to enable them to marry
59.	a	Clark
60.	a	*A Fantasy Actually Filmed in Northern Alaska*
61.	a	Haddon Sundblom
62.	b	He asked all the passengers to pray
63.	a	*Harper's Weekly*

Dickens
to the Grinch

tots to teens puzzlers

Sugar Plums

1. In the story *How the Grinch Stole Christmas,* who does the Grinch steal Christmas from?
   a. The Whats b. The Whos c. The Whys d. The Wheres

2. In the poem "A Visit from St. Nicholas," what do the children dream about?
   a. Presents b. Sugar plums c. Candy d. Chickens

3. When Little Jack Horner sticks his thumb into his Christmas pie, what does he find?
   a. A blackbird c. Curds and whey
   b. A plum d. Crust

4. In the story *A Christmas Carol,* what is Ebenezer Scrooge famous for saying?
   a. Boo diddlebug c. Bug dumrug
   b. Bah humbug d. Bing hatbug

5. According to the poem "A Visit from St. Nicholas," what does Santa's stomach do when he laughs?
   a. Shakes like a bowl full of jelly
   b. Quivers like a plate full of preserves
   c. Jiggles like a dish full of marmalade
   d. Wiggles like a jar full of jam

6. In the poem "A Visit from St. Nicholas," what is the jolly man wearing?
   a. Robes   b. Fur   c. A red suit   d. Nothing

7. What is the name of Bob Cratchit's sick child in *A Christmas Carol*?
   a. Little Nell   b. Baby Bobby   c. Tiny Tim   d. Wee Willy

8. In *How the Grinch Stole Christmas*, why is the Grinch so mean?
   a. His hat was two sizes too big   c. His shoes pinched his toes
   b. His heart was two sizes too small   d. He had a toothache

9. The gingerbread houses that have become popular at Christmastime were inspired by which fairy tale?
   a. *The Gingerbread Man*   c. *Hansel and Gretel*
   b. *Snow White*   d. *Little Red Riding Hood*

10. The story *Christmas with Anne* features which famous character?
    a. Queen Anne
    b. Anne of the Indies
    c. Anne of Green Gables
    d. Little Orphan Annie

11. Which of these is *not* one of the three ghosts who visits Scrooge in *A Christmas Carol*?
    a. Ghost of Christmas Past
    b. Ghost of Christmas Present
    c. Ghost of Christmas Yet to Come
    d. Ghost of Christmas Never Never

Candy Canes

12. The book *Christmas in the Big Igloo* chronicles Christmas celebrations in which part of North America?
    a. The Mexican desert
    b. The Pacific coast
    c. New York City
    d. The Canadian Arctic

13. In *A Christmas Carol*, what kind of bird does Scrooge send the young boy to the butcher shop to buy on Christmas morning?
    a. A goose   b. A duck   c. A turkey   d. A pheasant

14. In the classic Christmas fairy tale *The Fir Tree*, what does the tree wish to become?
    a. Round and fat
    b. Old and great
    c. A home for birds
    d. A mighty oak

15. What line is Tiny Tim famous for saying at the end of
A Christmas Carol?
   a. "To all a goodnight"   c. "God bless us, everyone"
   b. "Please sir, I want some more" d. "Thank you, Mr. Scrooge"

16. There's an old English nursery rhyme that begins: "Christmas is coming, the geese are getting fat. Please put a penny in an old man's hat." If you don't have a penny, what else will do?
   a. A farthing   b. A ha'penny   c. A shilling   d. A sixpence

17. According to the nursery rhyme that begins "Christmas is coming, the geese are getting fat," what will happen if you have nothing to put in the old man's hat?
   a. You won't receive any presents   c. You'll have bad luck
   b. You won't get any dinner   d. God will be asked to bless you

18. In the Harry Potter books by J.K. Rowling, which of these gifts does Harry Potter receive during his third Christmas at Hogwarts School of Witchcraft and Wizardry?
   a. An invisibility cloak   c. A book of spells
   b. A Firebolt broomstick   d. A pair of mismatched socks
   BONUS: Which present did Harry Potter receive during his first Christmas?

19. Who wrote the classic Christmas tale *The Little Match Girl*?
   a. Aesop   c. Charles Dickens
   b. Hans Christian Andersen d. J.K. Rowling

Peanut Brittle

20. Which Shakespearean play is thought to have been written about the Christmas season?
    a. *The Merry Wives of Windsor*   c. *Twelfth Night*
    b. *The Winter's Tale*   d. *A Midsummer Night's Dream*

21. In the story *The Birds' Christmas Carol,* what happens on Christmas morning?
    a. A baby was born
    b. The children fed their breakfast to the birds
    c. A pet turkey that was to be eaten was spared
    d. Flocks of birds gathered in the forest to celebrate the birth of Jesus

22. In the Canadian story *The True Meaning of Crumbfest,* by David Weale, what do the mice look forward to receiving at Christmastime every year?
    a. Presents from Santa   c. New mittens
    b. Warm apple cider   d. Leftover crumbs

23. The author of *Alice in Wonderland* also wrote a short poem called "Christmas Greeting from a Fairy to a Child." What is the author's name?
    a. Louisa May Alcott   c. A.A. Milne
    b. Lewis Carroll   d. Robert Frost

24. In the book *Little Women,* what gift do the March girls receive from their mother on Christmas morning?
    a. Dolls   b. Books   c. Hair ribbons   d. Candy

25. In the Christmas chapter of *The Wind in the Willows,* what kind of little creatures do Mole and Rat hear carolling?
    a. Rabbits   b. Kittens   c. Field mice   d. Chipmunks

26. Which famous children's author wrote *The Life and Adventures of Santa Claus*?
    a. Dr. Seuss   c. Judy Blume
    b. L. Frank Baum   d. Roald Dahl
    BONUS: For what children's book series is this author most famous?

27. The famous poet Dylan Thomas wrote "A Child's Christmas in …" what place?
    a. Florida   b. Wales   c. A toy store   d. Paris

28. In *A Christmas Carol,* Scrooge tells Marley's ghost that he thinks there is more *what* than grave about him?
    a. Gravity   b. Gravelox   c. Gravol   d. Gravy

Grown-ups' Brainteasers

Pumpkin Pies

29. Who is credited with writing the classic poem "A Visit from St. Nicholas"?
    a. Charles Dickens   c. Clement C. Moore
    b. Mark Twain   d. Louisa May Alcott

30. In *A Christmas Carol*, how long has Marley been dead?
    a. Seventeen years   c. Three years
    b. Seven years   d. Six months

31. Which bestselling author of legal thrillers wrote the book *Skipping Christmas*?
    a. Scott Turow   c. John Grisham
    b. Richard North Patterson d. Robert Ludlum

32. In the book *Little Women*, what Christmas gift does the March family give to their poor neighbours?
    a. Their own breakfast   c. A beautiful Christmas tree
    b. Hand-knit sweaters   d. A pumpkin pie

33. Which bestselling thriller writer switched to a different genre with a book titled *The Christmas Train*?
    a. Stephen King
    b. David Baldacci
    c. Clive Cussler
    d. James Patterson

34. Where were the Christmas revels immortalized in *The Pickwick Papers,* by Charles Dickens?
    a. Bob Cratchit's house
    b. Dingley Dell
    c. Fagin's loft
    d. The Tower of London

35. Who wrote the famous poem "Christmas Trees (A Christmas Circular Letter)"?
    a. T.S. Eliot
    b. Walt Whitman
    c. Ezra Pound
    d. Robert Frost

36. Who wrote the famous short story *The Gift of the Magi*?
    a. O. Henry   b. James Joyce   c. Oscar Wilde   d. Franz Kafka

pLum puddings

37. Everyone knows who wrote *How the Grinch Stole Christmas.* Or do they? What was Dr. Seuss's real name?
    a. William Winkle
    b. Theodor Geisel
    c. Franklin W. Dixon
    d. Albert Schmidt

38. In what year was *How the Grinch Stole Christmas* first published?
    a. 1936   b. 1944   c. 1957   d. 1968

39. What was the first children's book ever written by Dr. Seuss?
    a. *How the Grinch Stole Christmas*
    b. *And to Think That I Saw It on Mulberry Street*
    c. *Horton Hears a Who*
    d. *Green Eggs and Ham*

40. Besides writing *How the Grinch Stole Christmas* and other children's books, what else did Dr. Seuss do?
    a. Danced ballet   c. Wrote *New York Times* editorials
    b. Trained horses   d. Created military training videos

41. According to the story *The Life and Adventures of Santa Claus* by L. Frank Baum, what was the first toy Santa Claus ever made?
    a. A rag doll   b. A toy train   c. A wooden cat   d. A sled

42. What is the ending to the following quote by American scholar, educator, and author Mary Ellen Chase: "Christmas, children, is not a date. It is …"?
    a. A holiday   c. A world unto itself
    b. A state of mind   d. A present grab

43. What is the name of the first train on which journalist Tom Langdon travels in the novel *The Christmas Train*?
    a. The Capitol Limited   c. The Canadian
    b. The Orient Express   d. The Trans-Siberian

44. In 1843, Charles Dickens set the price of his new novel *A Christmas Carol* at an amount that would be affordable to everybody in England. How much did it cost?
    a. Five pence   b. Five shillings   c. Five pounds   d. Five farthings

45. In the preface to *A Christmas Carol,* what adjective does Charles Dickens use to describe his "little book"?
    a. Festive   b. Long-winded   c. Brilliant   d. Ghostly

Chestnuts

46. In what newspaper did the famous editorial containing the line "Yes, Virginia, there is a Santa Claus" first appear?
    a. *New York Times*   c. *New York Sun*
    b. *New York Herald*   d. *New York Post*

47. Which writer penned the famous "Yes, Virginia, there is a Santa Claus" editorial?
    a. Horace Greeley   c. Desmond Morris
    b. Francis P. Church   d. E.B. White

48. In what year did the editorial containing the line "Yes, Virginia, there is a Santa Claus" first appear?

    a. 1900   b. 1897   c. 1912   d. 1856

49. How old was Virginia when she wrote to a newspaper editor to ask if Santa Claus was real?

    a. Six   b. Seven   c. Eight   d. Nine

50. Who wrote "Dancing Dan's Christmas"?

    a. Sinclair Lewis   c. Damon Runyon
    b. John Steinbeck   d. Ernest Hemingway

51. Which of these is not a Christmas story written by Charles Dickens?

    a. *The Cricket on the Hearth*   c. *Yule Tidings*
    b. *The Chimes*   d. *The Pickwick Papers*

52. Clement C. Moore, author of the poem "A Visit from St. Nicholas," was what, for a living?

    a. A doctor   c. A journalist
    b. A literature professor d. An historian

53. Who wrote the first Christmas message to be broadcast by a British monarch?
   a. Winston Churchill
   b. Rudyard Kipling
   c. Randolph Churchill
   d. Virginia Wolff

54. Before he wrote children's books, which advertising slogan did Dr. Seuss create?
   a. Drano down the drain
   b. You'll wonder where the yellow went
   c. Quick Henry, the Flit
   d. Look sharp, feel sharp, be sharp

55. Where did the pen name Dr. Seuss come from?
   a. His mother's maiden name
   b. His wife's maiden name
   c. His grandmother's maiden name
   d. He made it up

56. In the short story *The Gift of the Magi*, what does Della, the young wife, buy her husband, Jim, for Christmas?
   a. A tie   b. Socks   c. A watch fob   d. A Bible

57. Dylan Thomas's poem "A Child's Christmas in Wales" was originally written as what?
   a. A radio script
   b. A story for his kids
   c. A screenplay
   d. A song

58. Which famous children's author wrote the poem "Christmas Greeting from a Fairy to a Child"?
   a. Lewis Carroll   c. J.M. Barrie
   b. C.S. Lewis   d. Louisa May Alcott

59. How many publishers initially rejected the bestseller *The Christmas Box*?
   a. Six   b. Thirteen   c. Twenty   d. None

answers

tots to teens puzzlers

Sugar Plums (1 point each)

1.	b	The Whos
2.	b	Sugar plums
3.	b	A plum
4.	b	Bah humbug
5.	a	Shakes like a bowl full of jelly
6.	b	Fur
7.	c	Tiny Tim
8.	b	His heart was two sizes too small
9.	c	*Hansel and Gretel*
10.	c	Anne of Green Gables
11.	d	Ghost of Christmas Never Never

CaNdy CaNes (2 points each)

12.	d	The Canadian Arctic
13.	c	A turkey
14.	b	Old and great
15.	c	"God bless us, everyone"
16.	b	A ha'penny
17.	d	God will be asked to bless you
18.	b	A Firebolt broomstick BONUS: An invisibility cloak
19.	b	Hans Christian Andersen

PeaNut BriTtLe (3 points each)

20.	c	*Twelfth Night*
21.	a	A baby was born
22.	d	Leftover crumbs
23.	b	Lewis Carroll
24.	b	Books
25.	c	Field mice
26.	b	L. Frank Baum BONUS: The Oz books
27.	b	Wales
28.	d	Gravy

Grown-ups' Brainteasers

Pumpkin Pies (1 point each)

29.	c	Clement C. Moore
30.	b	Seven years
31.	c	John Grisham
32.	a	Their own breakfast
33.	b	David Baldacci
34.	b	Dingley Dell
35.	d	Robert Frost
36.	a	O. Henry

Plum Puddings (2 points each)

37.	b	Theodor Geisel
38.	c	1957
39.	b	*And to Think That I Saw It on Mulberry Street*
40.	d	Created military training videos
41.	c	A wooden cat
42.	b	A state of mind
43.	a	The Capitol Limited
44.	b	Five shillings
45.	d	Ghostly

Chestnuts (3 points each)

46.	c	*New York Sun*
47.	b	Francis P. Church
48.	b	1897
49.	c	Eight
50.	c	Damon Runyon
51.	c	*Yule Tidings*
52.	b	A literature professor
53.	b	Rudyard Kipling
54.	c	Quick Henry, the Flit
55.	a	His mother's maiden name
56.	c	A watch fob
57.	a	A radio script
58.	a	Lewis Carroll
59.	a	Six

around the World

tots to teens puzzlers

Sugar Plums

1. What is the French word for Christmas?
   a. *Noël*   b. *Rendezvous*   c. *Café*   d. *Année*

2. Which Jewish holiday usually falls around the same time as Christmas?
   a. Passover   c. Rosh Hashanah
   b. Yom Kippur   d. Hanukkah

3. In which season does Christmas fall in South Africa?
   a. Spring   b. Summer   c. Fall   d. Winter
   BONUS: In which month does it fall?

4. What is the Swedish word for Christmas?
   a. Yul   b. Ikea   c. Volvo   d. Meatball

5. Instead of stockings, what article of clothing do French children leave out for Santa Claus to fill with gifts?
   a. Mittens   b. Shoes   c. Hats   d. Long underwear

6. In Ireland, it is a tradition to put what item in the window for the Holy Family?

   a. A pumpkin pie

   b. A candle

   c. A poinsettia

   d. A stocking

7. What is the German version of the carol "O Christmas Tree" called?

   a. "O Tannenbaum"

   b. "O Gesundheit"

   c. "O Dankeshein"

   d. "O Frankfurter"

8. In which U.S. state are you most likely not to have a white Christmas?

   a. Florida   b. New York   c. Minnesota   d. Vermont

9. In what language does "Feliz Navidad" mean "Merry Christmas"?

   a. French   b. Portuguese   c. Italian   d. Spanish

10. What kind of tree is often decorated for Christmas in Hawaii?

    a. A maple   b. An oak   c. A palm   d. A bonsai

Candy Canes

11. The French name for eggnog, *lait de poule,* literally means what?

    a. Chicken's milk

    b. Turkey's milk

    c. Eggy milk

    d. Rooster's milk

12. How do you say "Merry Christmas" in Argentina?
    a. Joyeux Noël   c. Felices Pasquas
    b. Kong He Xin Xi   d. Errymay Istmaschray

13. What stops for a few hours every Christmas Eve in Iceland?
    a. Clocks   b. TV   c. Santa's sleigh   d. Snowfall

14. On Christmas Eve 2000, what kind of snack did seven million
    children from the United Kingdom leave out for Santa Claus?
    a. Green eggs and ham   c. Pork chops and applesauce
    b. Mince pies and a drink   d. Wine and cheese

15. In Scotland, children have been known to "cry up the lum" at
    Christmastime. What does this mean?
    a. They throw tantrums for more presents
    b. They holler their wish lists up the chimney
    c. They stay up late to watch for Santa Claus
    d. They complain about the weather

16. In which European country might you eat a dish of *paella* at
    Christmastime?
    a. Sweden   b. Scotland   c. Switzerland   d. Spain

17. In rural Poland, Christmas Eve is traditionally a time for what
    activity?
    a. Swimming   c. Sunbathing
    b. Fortune-telling   d. Sneezing

18. Which European country holds the biggest Christmas lottery in the world, the *Loteria de Navidad*?
   a. Germany   b. Denmark   c. Spain   d. France

19. *Panettone* is a traditional Christmas dessert from which country?
   a. China   b. Egypt   c. Italy   d. Russia

20. *Glogg* is a Christmas tradition in Scandinavian countries at Christmastime. What is it?
   a. A drink   b. A decoration   c. A story   d. A gift

21. What is the traditional Christmas greeting on Christmas Island?
   a. Joyeux Noël   b. God Jul   c. Feliz Navidad   d. Merry Christmas

22. Which U.S. state is the last to welcome in a New Year?
   a. California   b. Arizona   c. Hawaii   d. New York

23. Which Canadian Christmas carol, sometimes known as "'Twas in the Moon of Wintertime," is named for a Native American tribe?
   a. "The Inuit Carol"   c. "The Blackfoot Carol"
   b. "The Iroquois Carol"   d. "The Huron Carol"

24. "An She Rock de Baby to Sleep" is a Christmas song in which North American country?
   a. United States   c. Jamaica
   b. Canada   d. Mexico

Peanut Brittle

25. In Australia, where chimneys are rare, through what does Santa Claus usually enter a house on Christmas Eve?
    a. The front door
    b. A window
    c. A wall
    d. A mouse hole

26. Which of these is a traditional Christmas Eve dish in Italy?
    a. Eel
    b. Pizza
    c. Rabbit
    d. Deer

27. Schmutzli, the companion to Switzerland's Saint Nicholas, threatens to do what to bad little children?
    a. Stuff them in his sack
    b. Make them eat dirt
    c. Kidnap their toys
    d. Cut off their noses

28. An integral part of Christmas celebrations in France is the *bûche de Noël*. What is it?
    a. A crepe shaped like a star
    b. A loaf of bread shaped like Santa's face
    c. A cake shaped like a yule log
    d. A gingerbread cookie shaped like an angel

29. In England, what do children do with their Christmas wish lists?
    a. Mail them to Father Christmas
    b. Put them under the Christmas tree
    c. Throw them in the fireplace
    d. Place them next to Santa's snack

30. What kind of fish makes up the traditional Christmas Eve dinner in Portugal?
    a. Trout   b. Cod   c. Salmon   d. Tuna

31. In Swedish folklore, what kind of animal carries the Yule Elf when he makes his rounds to deliver presents at Christmastime?
    a. Lion   b. Tiger   c. Bear   d. Goat

32. In China, Santa Claus is known as "Dun Che Lao Ren," which means what?
    a. Christmas old man   c. Large present-giver
    b. Fat red suit   d. Merry bearded one

33. According to folk tales of various European countries, Christmas Eve is a night of magic. Which of the following is believed to happen?
    a. People can become invisible
    b. Water turns to gold
    c. Animals can speak with human voices
    d. Children can fly

34. In Ukraine, which event must occur before Christmas dinner is served?
    a. All the presents are opened
    b. Every stomach in the room growls
    c. The first star appears in the sky
    d. The chorus of "Jingle Bells" is sung

35. *Kutya* is a traditional Ukrainian Christmas dish symbolizing life and prosperity. What is it?

    a. Cake   b. Stew   c. A sandwich   d. Porridge

36. In which U.S. state might you eat a fish pie called *piruk* for dessert on Christmas?

    a. Iowa   b. Montana   c. Texas   d. Alaska

37. Why did U.S. president Theodore Roosevelt ban Christmas trees from the White House when he was in office?

    a. He was allergic to them
    b. He disliked the smell of pine
    c. He was concerned for the environment
    d. He was worried they would catch fire

38. *Tourtière* is a traditional Christmas dish in Quebec. What is it?

    a. Sugar pie   b. Meat pie   c. Pumpkin pie   d. Cheese pie

39. What kind of meat might you serve for a traditional Christmas dinner in Jamaica?

    a. Goat   b. Buffalo   c. Reindeer   d. Aardvark

40. What is the name of the New York City hotel where the title character of *Eloise at Christmastime* lives?

    a. The Plaza   c. The Palace
    b. The Park Avenue   d. The Paramount

Grown-ups' Brainteasers

Pumpkin Pies

41. When it is Christmas morning in New Zealand, what day is it in North America?

    a. December 24   b. December 25   c. December 26   d. April 1

42. In Scotland, what is a "first-footer"?

    a. The person who leads the first New Year's dance
    b. The first person to enter a church for midnight services on Christmas Eve
    c. The first yule log bearer to enter the home
    d. The first person to enter the house after midnight on New Year's Eve
    BONUS: What do Scots traditionally give to a male "first-footer"?

43. Which country put a ban on Christmas between the years 1649 and 1660?

    a. France   b. Italy   c. England   d. Spain

44. In Poland, it is a Christmas Eve tradition for a young woman to eavesdrop on her neighbour's conversation. According to legend, if she overhears the word "go," what will happen to her in the coming year?

    a. She'll get good grades at school   c. She'll marry
    b. She'll travel far away   d. She'll win a lottery

45. What is London's main Christmas shopping street?
    a. Whitehall   c. Grosvenor Street
    b. Oxford Street   d. Fleet Street

46. The poinsettia plant was introduced into the United States and
    Canada from which country?
    a. Spain   b. Mexico   c. Brazil   d. Australia

47. Every Christmas, the Molly Brown House in Denver, Colorado,
    re-creates a Victorian Christmas, complete with candlelight tours
    and high teas. What is Molly Brown famous for?
    a. Discovering the first gold mine in Colorado
    b. Surviving the sinking of the *Titanic*
    c. Her accuracy with a rifle
    d. The first woman preacher west of the Mississippi River

48. Which New York City theatre is world-famous for its annual
    Christmas show?
    a. Carnegie Hall   c. Winter Garden
    b. Radio City Music Hall   d. Lincoln Center

49. Which late pop singer's home continues to be lavishly decorated
    for the holidays, carrying on a tradition he established at the
    height of his fame?
    a. John Lennon   b. Frank Sinatra   c. Dean Martin   d. Elvis Presley

50. For many years, Canadian-born band leader Guy Lombardo was a fixture on TV New Year's Eve celebrations. What was the name of his orchestra?
   a. Canadian Musicmakers   c. Royal Canadians
   b. Royal Musicians   d. Canadian Idols

51. In Mexico, the poinsettia plant was originally also known by what name?
   a. The flower of Christ   c. The flower of the Holy Night
   b. The flower of the Virgin d. The flower of Baby Jesus

pLum puõõiNgs

52. Eastern Orthodox Christians celebrate Christmas according to the Julian calendar. Who created the Julian calendar?
   a. Pope Julius I   b. St. Julian   c. Julius Caesar   d. Jove

53. What is the name for Santa Claus throughout most of the Middle East?
   a. Baba Noël   b. Abdulnik   c. Christoff   d. Peter Pita

54. How is December 23 known in Norway and Denmark?
   a. Christmas Eve Eve   c. Little Christmas Eve
   b. Early Eve   d. First Evening

55. In Europe, what are horses sometimes offered to drink on Christmas?

    a. Milk   b. Water   c. Beer   d. Wine

56. In the French region of Provence, how many desserts is it tradition to serve after Christmas Mass?

    a. Three   b. Seven   c. Ten   d. Thirteen

    BONUS: What do the desserts represent?

57. Who delivers Christmas presents to children in Austria?

    a. St. Nikolaus   c. St. Josef

    b. The Christkind   d. The Foehn

58. During his 2003 Christmas message, Pope John Paul II delivered Christmas greetings in how many languages?

    a. Over twenty   b. Over thirty   c. Over forty   d. Over fifty

59. How long is the celebration of Hanukkah?

    a. One day   b. Five days   c. Eight days   d. Twelve days

60. What language gave us the abbreviation "Xmas"?

    a. Latin   b. Russian   c. Greek   d. Hebrew

61. In 1992, what gift did U.S. vice-president Al Gore give to his wife, Tipper, for Christmas?

    a. A mink coat   b. Perfume   c. A drum set   d. A car

62. In Quebec, *réveillon* immediately follows midnight Mass. What is it?

    a. A dance   b. A toast   c. A song   d. A meal

63. What act of religious observance was practised by many francophone Canadians on Christmas Eve?

    a. Saying one thousand Hail Marys
    b. Reading the Gospel of St. Luke
    c. Reciting the Lord's Prayer one hundred times
    d. Praying for forgiveness in front of the family crèche

64. In St. Augustine, Florida, a city ordinance prevents anyone from displaying outdoor Christmas lights that are not what colour?

    a. Red   b. Green   c. White   d. Orange

65. Which is not the name of a real place in the state of Texas?

    a. Nazareth   c. Christmas Creek
    b. Santaville   d. Egg Nog Branch

Chestnuts

66. Christmas Island is administered by which country?

    a. Great Britain   b. Australia   c. New Zealand   d. South Africa

67. Who brings children gifts in Russia on Little Christmas?

    a. St. Nicholas   b. Baboushka   c. Baba Noël   d. St. Joseph

68. Ukrainians do not usually give gifts on Christmas Day but on which day?
   a. Little Christmas
   b. Christmas Eve
   c. Feast of St. Nicholas
   d. New Year's Day

69. What witchlike figure brings gifts to Italian children on Little Christmas?
   a. Barbarella   b. Barola   c. Befana   d. Boda

70. Whom does the spectacular Brazilian festival Folia de Reis honour?
   a. Mary and Joseph
   b. The Christ Child
   c. The Three Wise Men
   d. God

71. Las Posadas, a Latin American celebration commemorating Mary and Joseph's journey from Nazareth to Bethlehem, lasts for how long?
   a. Two days   b. Five days   c. Seven days   d. Nine days

72. In some cultures, it is a tradition to disguise oneself at Christmastime and go visiting door to door, seeking hospitality. Which of the following is not one of the various names for this custom?
   a. Belsnickling
   b. Mumming
   c. Guising
   d. Hobnobbing

73. In Denmark, what is December 26 also known as?
    a. Second Christmas   c. After Christmas
    b. Next Noël   d. Boxing Day

74. How is Baby Jesus known throughout Spanish America?
    a. El Niño   c. Il Christos
    b. Jesu Bambino   d. Feliz Navidad
    BONUS: What else is known by the same name?

75. In which Italian town is St. Nicholas buried?
    a. Brindisi   b. Bari   c. Braccagni   d. Brozzi

76. In Wales, what item is placed atop a pole and carried from house
    to house in the Christmas custom of *Mari Lwyd*?
    a. A lamb carcass   c. A demonic mask
    b. A horse's skull   d. An old shoe

77. In what city did the mayor personally burn Christmas
    decorations in the seventeenth century?
    a. Berlin   b. London   c. Paris   d. Madrid

78. According to Icelandic legend, what will happen to people who
    don't receive at least one new garment for Christmas?
    a. They'll get caught by the Christmas Cat
    b. They'll go cold
    c. They'll have a year of bad luck
    d. They'll get all of the Christmas pudding to themselves

79. At one time, it was customary in parts of the United Kingdom for a bell to toll one hour before midnight on Christmas Eve. What did this represent?

a. The appearance of the angels to the shepherds
b. The devil's funeral
c. The arrival of Mary and Joseph at the stable
d. The redemption of humankind

80. Which Scandinavian city sends a Christmas tree to London's Trafalgar Square every year?

a. Oslo   b. Helsinki   c. Lillehammer   d. Stockholm

81. In what year did the U.S. Congress seriously consider cancelling Christmas?

a. 1898   b. 1918   c. 1933   d. 1941

82. Every year, Lunenburg County, Nova Scotia, produces and ships thousands of which essential Christmas item?

a. Santa hats
b. Turkeys
c. Christmas trees
d. Nativity scenes

83. What holiday item was banned from Canadian airplanes during the 2003 Christmas season because of its potential to conceal a dangerous weapon?

a. Santa beards
b. Fruitcake
c. Christmas wreaths
d. Turkeys

84. In Newfoundland, what does the old custom of "blowing the pudding" involve when the Christmas pudding is lifted from the pot?
    a. A bagpipe solo
    b. Blowing of soap bubbles
    c. A whistling chorus
    d. Gunfire

85. Which was the first U.S. state to recognize December 25 as an official holiday?
    a. New York
    b. Virginia
    c. South Carolina
    d. Alabama

86. Which U.S. president displayed the Christmas Tree of Meat—an apple tree laden with gifts of turkeys, opossums, capons, ducks, and geese—in his backyard?
    a. Harry Truman
    b. George Washington
    c. Warren Harding
    d. Herbert Hoover

87. The word *danistayohihv* is associated with Christmas in the language of the Cherokee people. What does it mean?
    a. Beautiful tree
    b. Fat man with gifts
    c. Peace and love
    d. Firecrackers

88. Every year in Portugal, teams compete for the Santa Claus Cup. What is the sport?
    a. Basketball
    b. Soccer
    c. Polo
    d. Hockey

answers

tots to teens puzzlers

Sugar Plums (1 point each)

1.	a	Noël
2.	d	Hanukkah
3.	b	Summer BONUS: December
4.	a	Yul
5.	b	Shoes
6.	b	A candle
7.	a	"O Tannenbaum"
8.	a	Florida
9.	d	Spanish
10.	c	A palm

Candy Canes (2 points each)

11.	a	Chicken's milk
12.	c	Felices Pasquas

13.	b	TV
14.	b	Mince pies and a drink
15.	b	They holler their wish lists up the chimney
16.	d	Spain
17.	b	Fortune-telling
18.	c	Spain
19.	c	Italy
20.	a	A drink
21.	d	Merry Christmas
22.	c	Hawaii
23.	d	"The Huron Carol"
24.	c	Jamaica

Peanut Brittle (3 points each)

25.	b	A window
26.	a	Eel
27.	a	Stuff them in his sack
28.	c	A cake shaped like a yule log
29.	c	Throw them in the fireplace
30.	b	Cod
31.	d	Goat
32.	a	Christmas old man

33.	c	Animals can speak with human voices
34.	c	The first star appears in the sky
35.	d	Porridge
36.	d	Alaska
37.	c	He was concerned for the environment
38.	b	Meat pie
39.	a	Goat
40.	a	The Plaza

GROWN-UPS' BRAINTEASERS

Pumpkin Pies (1 point each)

41.	a	December 24
42.	d	The first person to enter the house after midnight on New Year's Eve BONUS: Whisky
43.	c	England
44.	c	She'll marry
45.	b	Oxford Street
46.	b	Mexico
47.	b	Surviving the sinking of the *Titanic*
48.	b	Radio City Music Hall
49.	d	Elvis Presley
50.	c	Royal Canadians
51.	c	The flower of the Holy Night

Plum Puddings (2 points each)

52.	c	Julius Caesar
53.	a	Baba Noël
54.	c	Little Christmas Eve
55.	c	Beer
56.	d	Thirteen BONUS: Christ and the twelve Apostles
57.	b	The Christkind
58.	d	Over fifty
59.	c	Eight days
60.	c	Greek (in the Greek alphabet, "X" is *chi*, the first letter of Christ's name)
61.	c	A drum set
62.	d	A meal
63.	a	Saying one thousand Hail Marys
64.	c	White
65.	b	Santaville

Chestnuts (3 points each)

66.	b	Australia
67.	b	Baboushka
68.	c	Feast of St. Nicholas (December 6)
69.	c	Befana
70.	c	The Three Wise Men
71.	d	Nine days

72.	d	Hobnobbing
73.	a	Second Christmas
74.	a	El Niño BONUS: A warming of Pacific waters
75.	b	Bari
76.	b	A horse's skull
77.	b	London
78.	a	They'll get caught by the Christmas Cat
79.	b	The devil's funeral
80.	a	Oslo
81.	b	1918
82.	c	Christmas trees
83.	b	Fruitcake
84.	d	Gunfire
85.	d	Alabama
86.	c	Warren Harding
87.	d	Firecrackers
88.	c	Polo

traditional
Christmas
Carols

tots to teens puzzlers

Sugar Plums

1. In "Away in a Manger," what wakes Baby Jesus?
   a. Sheep   b. Angels   c. Cattle   d. The TV

2. In "Silent Night," how is the night described?
   a. Soft and white   c. Calm and bright
   b. Clear and light   d. Peaceful and right

3. In "The Twelve Days of Christmas," which gift is received each day?
   a. Partridge in a pear tree   c. Turtle dove
   b. Calling bird   d. Box of chocolates

4. In "The Twelve Days of Christmas," who is sending all the gifts?
   a. My new love   c. My foolish love
   b. My true love   d. Santa Claus

5. Which of these birds is not mentioned in "The Twelve Days of Christmas"?
   a. Turtledove   b. Partridge   c. Swan   d. Ostrich

6. According to the carol, what came upon a midnight clear?
   a. The Three Wise Men   c. That glorious song of old
   b. Jolly old St. Nicholas   d. The little town of Bethlehem

7. According to "I Saw Three Ships," at what time on Christmas day did the ships come sailing in?
   a. Morning   b. Afternoon   c. Evening   d. Night

8. According to "Deck the Halls," what is Christmas the season to be?
   a. Merry   b. Happy   c. Jolly   d. Generous

9. In "Deck the Halls," what are the halls to be decked with?
   a. Boughs of holly   c. Corn and barley
   b. Poison ivy   d. Scrooge and Marley

10. In "Joy to the World," what are said to be singing?
    a. Rocks and hills   c. Heaven and nature
    b. Trees and plants   d. Dogs and cats

Candy Canes

11. Which Christmas carol asks the listener to "Join the triumph of the skies"?
    a. "The First Noël"   c. "Joy to the World"
    b. "Hark! The Herald Angels Sing"   d. "O Come All Ye Faithful"

12. Which two plants make up the name of a traditional English carol?

    a. Mistletoe and myrtle   c. Fir and fern

    b. Holly and ivy   d. Primrose and poinsettia

13. In the chorus of "O Holy Night," what are you asked to do?

    a. Rise up and sing   c. Stop all your sinning

    b. Listen and pray   d. Fall on your knees

14. How is the snow described in "Good King Wenceslas"?

    a. Deep and crisp and even   c. Clean and thick and crunchy

    b. Cold and white and icy   d. Light and soft and flaky

15. What are the angels singing in "Angels We Have Heard on High"?

    a. Gloria, in Excelsis Deo!   c. Adeste Fideles!

    b. Hallelujah!   d. O come let us adore Him!

16. Which Christmas carol contains the lyric "O star of wonder, star of night"?

    a. "We Wish You a Merry Christmas"

    b. "We Three Kings"

    c. "While Shepherds Watched Their Flocks"

    d. "What Child Is This?"

17. What are the nine ladies doing in "The Twelve Days of Christmas"?

    a. Leaping   b. Dancing   c. Eating   d. Chatting

18. How many "las" follow the "fa" in "Deck the Halls"?
    a. Six   b. Seven   c. Eight   d. Nine

19. In "We Wish You a Merry Christmas," what do the carollers insist they must have before they will leave? (There are two correct answers. BONUS: score 4 points if you get both right.)
    a. Wassail   c. Fruitcake
    b. Figgy pudding   d. Cup of good cheer

20. In "Good King Wenceslas," whom does the king speak to?
    a. The poor man   b. His page   c. A guard   d. His queen

Peanut Brittle

21. "Silent Night" was originally written in what language?
    a. English   b. French   c. German   d. Latin

22. What is a manger?
    a. A feeding trough   c. A wheelbarrow
    b. A barn   d. A bed

23. In "The Twelve Days of Christmas," what gift arrives on the tenth day?
    a. Ten ladies dancing   c. Ten lords a-leaping
    b. Ten drummers drumming   d. Ten pipers piping

24. "O Come All Ye Faithful" is often sung in what language that is no longer commonly spoken?
    a. Babylonian   b. Latin   c. Saxon   d. Sanskrit

25. In "Hark! The Herald Angels Sing," what does the word "hark" mean?
    a. Pray   b. Rejoice   c. Listen   d. Join in

26. In "The Huron Carol," how is the Christmas season described?
    a. The time of ice and snow   c. The season of the cold north wind
    b. The moon of wintertime   d. The days in which the land is white

27. How many times is the word "Hallelujah" repeated at the opening of the "Hallelujah Chorus"?
    a. Five   b. Seven   c. Eight   d. Ten
    BONUS: How many times is it repeated at the end?

28. Where are the shepherds in "While Shepherds Watched Their Flocks"?
    a. Standing on a hilltop   c. Leaning against a rock
    b. Seated on the ground   d. Walking through a valley

29. Who wrote the "Hallelujah Chorus"?
    a. Mozart   b. Beethoven   c. Handel   d. Wagner
    BONUS: What famous work is it from?

30. In Charles Dickens' story *A Christmas Carol,* which carol does Scrooge hear that makes him angry?
    a. "Joy to the World"
    b. "God Rest Ye Merry Gentlemen"
    c. "Deck the Halls"
    d. "I Saw Three Ships"

Grown-ups' Brainteasers

Pumpkin Pies

31. What is another name for the carol "O Come All Ye Faithful"?
    a. "Semper Peratus"   c. "Magna Carta"
    b. "Joyeaux Noël"   d. "Adeste Fideles"

32. The music to "What Child Is This?" is also known by what name?
    a. "Greensleeves" b. "Yellowshirts" c. "Whitegloves" d. "Redpants"

33. In the fourth verse of "We Three Kings," how is myrrh described?
    a. Incense   c. Beauty bright
    b. Bitter perfume   d. Spice of old

34. Many traditional Christmas carols cannot be attributed to a particular songwriter. Which of these English carols falls into that group?
    a. "The First Noël"
    b. "God Rest Ye Merry Gentlemen"
    c. "The Holly and the Ivy"
    d. All three

35. The melody of "Deck the Halls" is believed to be of what origin?
    a. Welsh   b. English   c. Scottish   d. Irish

36. In what modern country is the carol "Good King Wenceslas" set?
    a. Germany   b. Poland   c. Austria   d. Czech Republic

37. "Angels from the Realms of Glory" is also known by what name?
    a. "The Queen's Carol"   c. "Victorian Carol"
    b. "Westminster Carol"   d. "Brook's Carol"

38. Which of these is the name of a Christmas carol dating from the sixteenth century?
    a. "The Swan's Neck Carol"   c. "The Cat's Nose Carol"
    b. "The Fox Tail's Carol"   d. "The Boar's Head Carol"

39. Which rock-and-roll group recorded its own version of "Joy to the World"—with no reference whatsoever to Christmas?
    a. The Beatles   c. Cream
    b. Three Dog Night   d. The Monkees

40. In which country was the carol "Silent Night" written?

a. Germany   b. Austria   c. Switzerland   d. Prussia

Plum Puddings

41. What was the first Christmas carol written by an American that remains popular to this day?

a. "Joy to the World"   c. "It Came Upon a Midnight Clear"
b. "Away in a Manger"   d. "Hark! The Herald Angels Sing"

42. Which country did Good King Wenceslas rule during his lifetime?

a. Greece   b. Romania   c. Bohemia   d. Macedonia

43. How many presents would you have if you received all the gifts in "The Twelve Days of Christmas"?

a. 164   b. 264   c. 364   d. 464

44. On what day of the year does Good King Wenceslas see the poor man gathering winter fuel?

a. December 25   b. December 26   c. January 1   d. January 6

45. Who is known as the Father of Carolling because he encouraged churchgoers to join in Christmas hymn-singing at a time when the practice was limited to clergy?

a. Martin Luther   c. St. Nicholas
b. St. Francis of Assisi   d. Pope Clement IV

46. The first published version of "The Twelve Days of Christmas" was in a book of children's nursery rhymes. What was the year?
    a. 1639   b. 1780   c. 1815   d. 1903

47. In what city was "O Little Town of Bethlehem" written?
    a. Jerusalem   c. Philadelphia
    b. London   d. Athens

48. What was the first musical instrument on which "Silent Night" was played?
    a. Guitar   b. Violin   c. Harpsichord   d. Lute

49. The words to "I Heard the Bells on Christmas Day" were written by one of the most famous poets of the nineteenth century. Who was it?
    a. Samuel Taylor Coleridge   c. Henry Wadsworth Longfellow
    b. Robert Browning   d. Walt Whitman

50. Which two women's names complete the title of the French carol "Bring a Torch …"?
    a. Anne and Nathalie   c. Sandrine and Marie
    b. Jeanette and Isabella   d. Nicole and Monique

51. In what country was "We Three Kings" written?
    a. England   b. Cyprus   c. United States   d. Egypt

52. The words to "O Holy Night" were written in France in 1847 by
    Placide Clappeau, the mayor of the town of Roquemaure. What
    was his occupation?
    a. Tavern keeper   c. Farmer
    b. Wine merchant   d. Baker

53. Good King Wenceslas was a real person. In what year was he
    born?
    a. 622 A.D.   b. 907 A.D.   c. 1286 A.D.   d. 1345 A.D.

54. How old was Good King Wenceslas when he died?
    a. Twenty-two   b. Thirty-six   c. Fifty-eight   d. Ninety-three

55. George Frederic Handel is most famous for his oratorio
    The Messiah, which is frequently performed during the
    Christmas season. But he also wrote the music to a
    popular Christmas carol. What is it?
    a. "Silent Night"
    b. "While Shepherds Watched Their Flocks"
    c. "I Saw Three Ships"
    d. "Hark! The Herald Angels Sing"

56. The Latin words to "Adeste Fideles" were written by a composer of what nationality?

    a. French   b. Italian   c. British   d. German

57. "O Come All Ye Faithful" was for many years known by what other name in England?

    a. "The Roman Ode"   c. "The Call to Worship"
    b. "The Portuguese Hymn"   d. "The Gathering"

58. In ancient times, holly was said to represent men and ivy to represent women. What do they represent in the carol "The Holly and the Ivy"?

    a. God and mankind   c. Jesus and Mary
    b. Joseph and Mary   d. God and Jesus

59. For many years, the authors of "Silent Night" were unknown. Their names were learned only after an order was given to court musicians to search them out. Who gave the order?

    a. The czar of Russia   c. The king of Prussia
    b. The pope   d. The queen of England

60. What was the profession of the author of the lyrics of "Angels from the Realms of Glory"?

    a. Priest   c. University professor
    b. Newspaper publisher   d. Orchestra conductor

answers

tots to teens puzzlers

Sugar Plums (1 point each)

1.	c	Cattle
2.	c	Calm and bright
3.	a	Partridge in a pear tree
4.	b	My true love
5.	d	Ostrich
6.	c	That glorious song of old
7.	a	Morning
8.	c	Jolly
9.	a	Boughs of holly
10.	c	Heaven and nature

Candy Canes (2 points each)

11.	b	"Hark! The Herald Angels Sing"
12.	b	Holly and ivy
13.	d	Fall on your knees
14.	a	Deep and crisp and even

15.	a	Gloria, in Excelsis Deo!
16.	b	"We Three Kings"
17.	b	Dancing
18.	c	Eight
19.	b & d	Figgy pudding; Cup of good cheer
		(Score 2 points for each correct answer.)
20.	b	His page

Peanut Brittle (3 points each)

21.	c	German
22.	a	A feeding trough
23.	c	Ten lords a-leaping
24.	b	Latin
25.	c	Listen
26.	b	The moon of wintertime
27.	d	Ten BONUS: Five
28.	b	Seated on the ground
29.	c	Handel BONUS: *The Messiah*
30.	b	"God Rest Ye Merry Gentlemen"

Grown-ups' Brainteasers

Pumpkin Pies (1 point each)

31.	d	"Adeste Fideles"
32.	a	"Greensleeves"
33.	b	Bitter perfume
34.	d	All three
35.	a	Welsh
36.	d	Czech Republic
37.	b	"Westminster Carol"
38.	d	"The Boar's Head Carol"
39.	b	Three Dog Night
40.	b	Austria

Plum Puddings (2 points each)

41.	c	"It Came Upon a Midnight Clear"
42.	c	Bohemia
43.	c	364
44.	b	December 26 (The Feast of Stephen)
45.	b	St. Francis of Assisi
46.	b	1780
47.	c	Philadelphia
48.	a	Guitar

49. c Henry Wadsworth Longfellow
50. b Jeanette and Isabella

Chestnuts (3 points each)

51. c United States
52. b Wine merchant
53. b 907 A.D.
54. a Twenty-two
55. b "While Shepherds Watched Their Flocks"
56. c British
57. b "The Portuguese Hymn"
58. c Jesus and Mary
59. c The king of Prussia
60. b Newspaper publisher

CHRISTMAS POPS

tots to teens puzzlers

Sugar Plums

1. Alvin is the star performer in which group?
   a. The Monkees   c. The Muppets
   b. The Chipmunks   d. The Reindeer

2. Whom does the Nutcracker fight with in *The Nutcracker Suite*?
   a. Sugar Plum Fairy   c. Flowers
   b. Mouse King   d. Dolls

3. In the song "Frosty the Snowman," what are Frosty's eyes made of?
   a. Coal   b. Snow   c. Dough   d. Pineapples

4. What makes Frosty the Snowman come to life?
   a. Corn cob pipe   c. Magic wand
   b. Old silk hat   d. Button eyes

5. In the first line of "Santa Claus Is Coming to Town," what are children advised not to do?
   a. Moan and sigh   c. Pout and cry
   b. Cheat and lie   d. Sit and spy

6. In "I Saw Mommy Kissing Santa Claus," where was Santa when Mommy kissed him?
   a. On the stairs
   c. In the chimney
   b. Underneath the mistletoe
   d. By the Christmas tree

7. According to the lyrics of "I Saw Mommy Kissing Santa Claus," what else did Mommy do to Santa besides kiss him?
   a. Danced with him
   c. Tickled him
   b. Gave him a present
   d. Fed him a cookie

8. Who gets run over by a reindeer in the popular song by Elmo & Patsy?
   a. Santa Claus
   c. Frosty the Snowman
   b. Grandma
   d. Uncle Jim

9. In "All I Want for Christmas Is My Two Front Teeth," why does the little boy want teeth for Christmas?
   a. So he can eat his broccoli
   b. So he can wish you Merry Christmas
   c. So he can smile
   d. So he can go to the dentist

10. What is *The Nutcracker*?
    a. A book   b. A ballet   c. An opera   d. A poem

Candy Canes

11. In "Up on the Housetop," what gift does Santa give Little Nell?
    a. A whip that cracks   c. A ball
    b. A dolly that laughs and cries   d. A lump of coal

12. What is the name of the little girl in *The Nutcracker*?
    a. Clara   b. Bella   c. Lisa   d. Anna

13. In the second verse of "Frosty the Snowman," what is in Frosty's hand when he runs down to the village?
    a. A carrot   b. A hat   c. A broomstick   d. A cookie

14. In "Go Tell It on the Mountain," what is it we are told to tell?
    a. Peace on earth   c. God is with us all
    b. Jesus Christ is born   d. Christmas Day is here

15. What holiday season song contains the line "Gone away is the bluebird"?
    a. "Blue Christmas"   c. "The Little Drummer Boy"
    b. "Winter Wonderland"   d. "I'll Be Home for Christmas"

16. What question does the Christmas song "Old Toy Trains" pose to the little boy?
    a. What do you want for Christmas?
    b. Don't you think it's time you were in bed?
    c. Have you been good this year?
    d. What colour is Rudolph's nose?

17. According to the 1950s hit, what colour was Elvis Presley's Christmas?
    a. White   b. Green   c. Yellow   d. Blue

18. In "The Chipmunk Song," Alvin says he wants only one thing for Christmas. What is it?
    a. A rubber ducky   c. A loop-the-loop
    b. A Hula Hoop   d. A sailboat

19. How many times is the word "Christmas" used in "Jingle Bells"?
    a. None   b. One   c. Five   d. Ten

20. What time is the clock striking in the second verse of "Jolly Old St. Nicholas"?
    a. Twelve   b. One   c. Two   d. Three

Peanut Brittle

21. Who popularized the song "Rudolph the Red-Nosed Reindeer"?
    a. Bing Crosby
    c. Gene Autry
    b. Hoagy Carmichael
    d. Nat King Cole

22. What is the name of the woman who goes for the sleigh ride in "Jingle Bells"?
    a. Little Nell   b. Fannie Bright   c. Mary Reilly   d. Doris Day

23. Who wrote *The Nutcracker Suite*?
    a. Rachmaninov
    c. Mussorgsky
    b. Rimsky-Korsakov
    d. Tchaikovsky

24. In "Toyland," the children who dwell there are described as being what?
    a. Full of joy
    c. Ever happy
    b. Always young
    d. Desperate to escape

25. According to "The Christmas Song," what kind of nuts should you be roasting on an open fire?
    a. Walnuts   b. Peanuts   c. Chestnuts   d. Brazil nuts

26. In "Do You Hear What I Hear?" whom does the little lamb pass a message to?
    a. The shepherd boy
    b. The mighty king
    c. The night wind
    d. The people everywhere

27. According to "Parade of the Wooden Soldiers," where does the parade take place?
    a. Around the Christmas tree
    b. In the children's bedroom
    c. In a toy shop
    d. In front of Santa Claus

28. Santa will know which stocking belongs to the singer of "Jolly Old St. Nicholas" because it is what?
    a. The longest one
    b. The shortest one
    c. The striped one
    d. The smelly one

29. Which of these is not part of *The Nutcracker*?
    a. "Waltz of the Flowers"
    b. "Dance of the Sugar Plum Fairy"
    c. "Russian Dance"
    d. "Mouseketeer Song"

30. The tale of *Rudolph the Red-Nosed Reindeer* originally began as what?
    a. A song
    b. A poem
    c. A short story
    d. A children's book

Grown-ups' Brainteasers

Pumpkin Pies

31. What is the title of the song that begins "Chestnuts roasting on an open fire"?
    a. "I'll Be Home for Christmas"   c. "Christmas in the City"
    b. "The Christmas Song"   d. "Silver Bells"

32. According to the lyrics of "White Christmas," in what city is the dreamer?
    a. San Francisco   b. Paris   c. Beverly Hills   d. Miami

33. Who wrote "White Christmas"?
    a. George Gershwin   c. Ira Gershwin
    b. Irving Berlin   d. Oscar Hammerstein II

34. Which of these artists did not record a version of "Santa Claus Is Coming to Town"?
    a. Bruce Springsteen   c. Bing Crosby
    b. Frank Sinatra   d. Kurt Cobain

35. Which of the following completes the title of the song "Happy Christmas …" written by John Lennon?
    a. Merry New Year   c. War Is Over
    b. Number Nine   d. And to All a Goodnight

36. Which 1970s group recorded "Merry Christmas Darling"?
   a. Captain & Tennille   c. The Bee Gees
   b. The Carpenters   d. Pink Floyd

37. For which Christmas favourite is Nat King Cole best known?
   a. "White Christmas"   c. "Silver Bells"
   b. "The Christmas Song"   d. "Christmas Dreaming"

38. Who introduces "Silver Bells" in the movie *The Lemon Drop Kid*?
   a. Margaret O'Brien   c. Bob Hope
   b. Bing Crosby   d. Rosemary Clooney

39. What author of a hit Broadway show wrote "It's Beginning to Look a Lot Like Christmas"?
   a. Richard Rodgers   c. Meredith Willson
   b. Oscar Hammerstein II   d. Irving Berlin
   BONUS: What was the hit show?

40. What group of British pop stars recorded "Do They Know It's Christmas?" to raise money for African famine relief?
   a. Food for All   b. Band Aid   c. Help Line   d. Pop Cares

Plum Puddings

41. In which of these songs is the word "Christmas" never used?
    a. "The Chipmunk Song"   c. "Up on the Housetop"
    b. "Home for the Holidays" d. "Rudolph the Red-Nosed Reindeer"

42. What is the only Christmas song that has ever been number one on the pop charts in the United States on Christmas Day?
    a. "Jingle Bells"
    b. "Santa Claus Is Coming to Town"
    c. "The Chipmunk Song"
    d. "Rudolph the Red-Nosed Reindeer"

43. Which of these Christmas songs was written first?
    a. "Jingle Bells"   c. "Away in a Manger"
    b. "Frosty the Snowman"   d. "O Little Town of Bethlehem"

44. Who popularized "Jingle Bell Rock"?
    a. Buddy Holly   b. Bobby Helms   c. Ricky Nelson   d. Elvis Presley

45. Which 1980s pop group recorded "White Christmas"?
    a. Culture Club   c. Wham!
    b. Thompson Twins   d. Duran Duran

46. Which Motown star had a 1976 hit with "What Christmas Means to Me"?
   a. Diana Ross
   b. Smokey Robinson
   c. Stevie Wonder
   d. Marvin Gaye

47. Which of the four ex-Beatles had a solo hit with "Wonderful Christmas Time"?
   a. John Lennon
   b. Paul McCartney
   c. George Harrison
   d. Ringo Starr

48. Which of these items is not requested for Christmas in "Santa Baby"?
   a. A deed to a platinum mine
   b. A yacht
   c. A private jet
   d. A light blue convertible

49. Which famous rock star performed the Christmas duet "Peace on Earth/Little Drummer Boy" with Bing Crosby in 1977?
   a. David Bowie
   b. Freddie Mercury
   c. Mick Jagger
   d. Elton John

50. In the 1950s, Nat King Cole sang about "The Little Boy That Santa Claus …"
   a. Loved
   b. Forgot
   c. Grew into
   d. Hugged

Chestnuts

51. What colour is the horse in "Jingle Bells"?
    a. Black   b. Brown   c. Bay   d. Blue

52. In "There's No Place Like Home for the Holidays," where is the man from Tennessee going?
    a. Florida   b. California   c. Pennsylvania   d. Nevada
    BONUS: What was he going to eat when he got there?

53. What musical group produced a version of *The Nutcracker* with lyrics in the 1940s?
    a. The Glenn Miller Orchestra   c. Spike Jones and His City Slickers
    b. The London Philharmonic   d. The Andrews Sisters

54. What song is on the flip side of the original 1957 Decca release of *Jingle Bell Rock*?
    a. "Captain Santa Claus (And His Reindeer Space Patrol)"
    b. "Big Rock Candy Mountain"
    c. "Blue Christmas"
    d. "I Saw Mommy Kissing Santa Claus"

55. The popular children's song "Up on the Housetop" was written in which period?
    a. 1850s   b. 1890s   c. Early 1900s   d. 1920s

56. What popular comedian of the day introduced the song "Santa Claus Is Coming to Town" on his radio show in 1934?
    a. Jack Benny   b. Fred Allen   c. George Burns d. Eddie Cantor

57. Who first recorded "Winter Wonderland"?
    a. Bing Crosby   c. Guy Lombardo
    b. Louis Armstrong   d. Percy Faith

58. Besides "White Christmas," what other Christmas song was introduced in the movie *Holiday Inn*?
    a. "There's No Place Like Home for the Holidays"
    b. "Have Yourself a Merry Little Christmas"
    c. "Happy Holidays"
    d. "I'll Be Home for Christmas"

59. What famous singer is co-author of "The Christmas Song"?
    a. Tony Bennett   c. Nat King Cole
    b. Mel Tormé   d. Paul Anka

60. What singer made "Rockin' Around the Christmas Tree" a hit?
    a. Teresa Brewer b. Janis Joplin   c. Brenda Lee   d. Carly Simon

answers

tots to teens puzzlers

Sugar Plums (1 point each)

1.	b	The Chipmunks
2.	b	Mouse King
3.	a	Coal
4.	b	Old silk hat
5.	c	Pout and cry
6.	b	Underneath the mistletoe
7.	c	Tickled him
8.	b	Grandma
9.	b	So he can wish you Merry Christmas
10.	b	A ballet

Candy Canes (2 points each)

11.	b	A dolly that laughs and cries
12.	a	Clara
13.	c	A broomstick
14.	b	Jesus Christ is born

15.	b	"Winter Wonderland"
16.	b	Don't you think it's time you were in bed?
17.	d	Blue
18.	b	A Hula Hoop
19.	a	None
20.	a	Twelve

Peanut Brittle (3 points each)

21.	c	Gene Autry
22.	b	Fannie Bright
23.	d	Tchaikovsky
24.	c	Ever happy
25.	c	Chestnuts
26.	a	The shepherd boy
27.	c	In a toy shop
28.	b	The shortest one
29.	d	"Mouseketeer Song"
30.	b	A poem

Grown-ups' Brainteasers

Pumpkin Pies (1 point each)

31.	b	"The Christmas Song"
32.	c	Beverly Hills
33.	b	Irving Berlin
34.	d	Kurt Cobain
35.	c	War Is Over
36.	b	The Carpenters
37.	b	"The Christmas Song"
38.	c	Bob Hope
39.	c	Meredith Willson BONUS: The Music Man
40.	b	Band Aid

Plum Puddings (2 points each)

41.	b	"Home for the Holidays"
42.	c	"The Chipmunk Song"
43.	a	"Jingle Bells"
44.	b	Bobby Helms
45.	c	Wham!
46.	c	Stevie Wonder
47.	b	Paul McCartney

48.	c	A private jet
49.	a	David Bowie
50.	b	Forgot

CHestNuts (3 points each)

51.	c	Bay
52.	c	Pennsylvania BONUS: Homemade pumpkin pie
53.	c	Spike Jones and His City Slickers
54.	a	"Captain Santa Claus (And His Reindeer Space Patrol)"
55.	a	1850s
56.	d	Eddie Cantor
57.	c	Guy Lombardo
58.	c	"Happy Holidays"
59.	b	Mel Torme
60.	c	Brenda Lee

tHE SiLVER SCREEN

tots to teens puzzlers

Sugar Plums

1. In which Christmas movie does an eight-year-old boy defend his home against burglars?
   a. *Miracle on 34th Street*
   b. *A Christmas Carol*
   c. *Home Alone*
   d. *It's a Wonderful Life*

2. What is the name of the head elf in *The Santa Clause*?
   a. Bernard
   b. Benjamin
   c. Bon-bon
   d. Bodacious

3. What do Huey, Dewey, and Louie wish for in *Mickey's Once Upon a Christmas*?
   a. For Santa to come
   b. That it was Christmas every day
   c. For lots of presents
   d. For Uncle Donald to come home

4. In which city is *Miracle on 34th Street* set?
   a. Philadelphia
   b. Chicago
   c. Los Angeles
   d. New York

5. Which of Santa's reindeer is the title subject of a 1989 movie?
   a. Dasher
   b. Dancer
   c. Prancer
   d. Vixen

6. In *Mickey's Christmas Carol*, which character plays the role of Ebenezer Scrooge?
   a. Scrooge McDuck
   b. Meanie Mouse
   c. Goofinezer
   d. Miserly Mickey

7. In *Mickey's Christmas Carol*, what role does Mickey Mouse play?
   a. Marley's Ghost
   b. Tiny Tim
   c. Bob Cratchit
   d. Uncle Fezziwig

8. In *The Christmas Toy*, which famous Muppet narrates the part of Santa Claus?
   a. Miss Piggy
   b. Fozzie
   c. Kermit the Frog
   d. Gonzo

Candy Canes

9. In the classic movie *Miracle on 34th Street*, where did Kris Kringle work?
   a. Bloomingdale's
   b. Gimbel's
   c. Macy's
   d. Wal-Mart

10. What famous actor who became a U.S. state governor plays the busy father in *Jingle All the Way?*
    a. Bruce Willis
    b. Pierce Brosnan
    c. George Clooney
    d. Arnold Schwarzenegger

11. In *The Muppet Christmas Carol,* which Muppet makes a guest appearance as Charles Dickens?
    a. Kermit the Frog
    b. Fozzie
    c. Gonzo
    d. Miss Piggy

12. In *A Christmas Story,* who eats the Christmas turkey?
    a. Ralphie
    b. Santa Claus
    c. The Bumpus's dogs
    d. The Grinch

13. In *Olive the Other Reindeer,* what kind of animal is Olive?
    a. A sheep   b. A moose   c. A dog   d. A cat

14. Who stars in the 2000 movie version of *How the Grinch Stole Christmas*?
    a. Bill Cosby
    b. Jim Carrey
    c. John Goodman
    d. Mike Myers

15. In *A Christmas Story,* what present does little Ralphie want the most?
    a. Lego   b. A robot   c. A BB gun   d. A bike

16. The first full-length animated movie created by Walt Disney was released just before Christmas 1937. What was it?
    a. *Fantasia*   b. *Bambi*   c. *Snow White*   d. *Cinderella*

17. In *The Santa Clause 2,* what does the second clause in the contract require that Santa do?
    a. Get married
    b. Build a new workshop
    c. Move to the South Pole
    d. Find a replacement Santa

18. What is the name of the Scrooge character in *An All Dogs Christmas Carol*?
    a. Belladonna
    b. Carface
    c. Cruella DeVil
    d. Charlie

Peanut Brittle

19. What classic story is the final segment of *Mickey's Once Upon a Christmas* based on?
    a. *A Christmas Carol*
    b. *How the Grinch Stole Christmas*
    c. *The Gift of the Magi*
    d. *A Visit from St. Nicholas*

20. In the 1997 movie *Beauty and the Beast: The Enchanted Christmas,* what is the name of the Christmas tree angel?
    a. Angelique   b. Chantal   c. Giselle   d. Marie

21. According to *The Christmas Toy*, what will happen to a toy if its secret ability to move when humans aren't around is discovered?
    a. The toy will become human
    b. The toy will be returned to the store
    c. The toy will become frozen forever
    d. The child won't love it anymore

22. In *Olive the Other Reindeer*, which of Santa's reindeer has a broken leg?
    a. Vixen   b. Blitzen   c. Comet   d. Cupid

23. Which well-loved children's television characters are named after the taxi driver and the cop in the Christmas classic *It's a Wonderful Life*?
    a. Mickey and Minnie   c. Daffy and Daisy
    b. Kermit and Fozzie   d. Bert and Ernie

24. What is the name of the little boy who is left at home by his parents in *Home Alone*?
    a. Karl   b. Ken   c. Kasper   d. Kevin

25. Which of these children's characters does not have a movie version of *A Christmas Carol* named after them?
    a. The Flintstones   c. Mickey Mouse
    b. The Muppets   d. Barney

26. Which actor plays the role of Kris Kringle in the original movie version of *Miracle on 34th Street*?

a. Monty Woolley

b. Edmund Gwenn

c. Charles Laughton

d. Lionel Barrymore

27. Benji got to star in his own Christmas movie, called *Benji's Very Own Christmas Story*. What is Benji?

a. A cat   b. A dog   c. A mouse   d. A horse

Grown-ups' Brainteasers

Pumpkin Pies

28. In *It's a Wonderful Life,* what happens every time a bell rings?

a. A child does a good deed

b. A new baby is born

c. An angel gets its wings

d. Dinner is served

29. Which actor never played Scrooge in a movie?

a. Sean Connery

b. Patrick Stewart

c. George C. Scott

d. Henry Winkler

30. Who supplies the voice of Mr. Magoo in *Mr. Magoo's Christmas Carol*?

a. Bill Cosby

b. George Burns

c. Jim Backus

d. Marlon Brando

31. Which movie star introduced the song "Have Yourself a Merry Little Christmas"?
    a. Barbra Streisand
    b. Judy Garland
    c. Marilyn Monroe
    d. Vera Ellen

32. Who plays Bing Crosby's love interest in *White Christmas*?
    a. Vera Ellen
    b. Dorothy Lamour
    c. Rosemary Clooney
    d. Sophia Loren

33. How many DVD listings appeared under the key word "Christmas" on Amazon.com in November 2003?
    a. 26   b. 93   c. 172   d. 343

34. Who plays the role of Kris Kringle in the 1994 remake of *Miracle on 34th Street*?
    a. Richard Harris
    b. Richard Attenborough
    c. Richard Burton
    d. Ralph Richardson

35. Which British actor plays the role of an elf in *Santa Claus: The Movie*?
    a. Anthony Hopkins
    b. John Cleese
    c. Dudley Moore
    d. Alec Guinness

36. In a 1964 film, who does Santa Claus conquer?
    a. The Grinch
    b. The Martians
    c. The Moon Kids
    d. The Mouse King

37. Which one-time Disney animator created *The Nightmare Before Christmas*?
    a. Tim Burton   c. Timothy Leary
    b. Tim Robbins   d. Tim Horton

38. In *A Christmas Story*, what is young Ralphie repeatedly warned will happen if he gets his one Christmas wish?
    a. He'll lose his allowance   c. He'll get sick to his stomach
    b. He'll shoot his eye out   d. He'll turn into a frog

Plum Puddings

39. In what movie did the song "White Christmas" debut?
    a. *It's a Wonderful Life*   c. *White Christmas*
    b. *Holiday Inn*   d. *I'll Be Home for Christmas*
    BONUS: What year was the movie released?

40. Which actor does not appear in the movie *White Christmas*?
    a. Donald O'Connor   c. Bing Crosby
    b. Danny Kaye   d. Dean Jagger

41. Which actor starred in a musical version of *A Christmas Carol* in 1970?
    a. Albert Finney   b. Bing Crosby   c. Bill Murray   d. Fred Astaire

42. Which young star plays the role of the disbelieving child in the original version of *Miracle on 34th Street*?
    a. Elizabeth Taylor   c. Judy Garland
    b. Natalie Wood   d. Shirley Temple

43. Who narrates the animated movie *Madeline's Christmas*?
    a. Laurence Olivier   c. Christopher Plummer
    b. Maurice Chevalier   d. Alistair Sim

44. In what movie did the song "Have Yourself a Merry Little Christmas" debut?
    a. *White Christmas*   c. *Meet Me in St. Louis*
    b. *I'll Be Home for Christmas*   d. *Annie*

45. Who narrates the animated movie *Santa Claus Is Coming to Town*?
    a. Bing Crosby   b. Bob Hope   c. Gene Kelly   d. Fred Astaire

46. Which of the following does not provide a voice for one of the characters in the 1998 version of *Rudolph the Red-Nosed Reindeer*?
    a. Dan Aykroyd   c. Debbie Reynolds
    b. Whoopi Goldberg   d. Bob Newhart

47. In *A Christmas Story*, where do Ralphie and his family eat Christmas dinner?
    a. Grandma's house
    b. In the living room beside their tree
    c. With the Bumpus family
    d. At a Chinese restaurant

48. In *A Family Man*, Nicolas Cage's character wakes up Christmas morning to find himself where?
    a. At the North Pole
    b. In someone else's home
    c. In a Santa Claus suit
    d. In Victorian England

49. Which classic holiday movie went into general release on Christmas Day 1946?
    a. *It's a Wonderful Life*
    b. *Miracle on 34th Street*
    c. *Holiday Inn*
    d. *White Christmas*

50. Which Academy Award–winning actor voices the part of Ebenezer Scrooge in *The Muppet Christmas Carol*?
    a. Dustin Hoffman
    b. Clint Eastwood
    c. Michael Caine
    d. Tom Hanks

Chestnuts

51. Which of the following unlikely people portrayed Santa Claus in a movie?
    a. Red Skelton
    b. Hulk Hogan
    c. Babe Ruth
    d. Rev. Jesse Jackson

52. How many Academy Awards did the original version of *Miracle on 34th Street* win?
    a. One
    b. Two
    c. Three
    d. None

53. Two of the following Christmas songs are heard in the movie *The Godfather*. Which are they? (There are two correct answers. Score 3 points for each correct answer; subtract 3 points for each incorrect answer.)
    a. "Rudolph the Red-Nosed Reindeer"
    b. "Santa Claus Is Coming to Town"
    c. "The Little Drummer Boy"
    d. "Have Yourself a Merry Little Christmas"

54. Who stars in *Mrs. Santa Claus*?
    a. Nicole Kidman
    b. Katharine Hepburn
    c. Angela Lansbury
    d. Carol Burnett

55. The first Christmas movie is believed to be a five-minute silent film that was released in 1901. What is its name?
   a. *A Trap for Santa*
   b. *A Holiday Pageant at Home*
   c. *Santa Claus vs. Cupid*
   d. *The Adventures of the Wrong Santa Claus*

56. Who plays the title character in *Richie Rich's Christmas Wish*?
   a. Macaulay Culkin
   b. Haley Joel Osment
   c. David Gallagher
   d. Dan Lauria

57. Which satirical Monty Python movie tells the story of the messiah?
   a. *The Life of Brian*
   b. *The Meaning of Life*
   c. *The Holy Grail*
   d. *The Flying Circus*

58. Which child star said the following: "I stopped believing in Santa Claus when I was six. Mother took me to see him in a department store and he asked for my autograph."
   a. Elizabeth Taylor
   b. Natalie Wood
   c. Judy Garland
   d. Shirley Temple

59. *Catch Me If You Can* opens on Christmas Eve 1969 in a prison in which city?

a. New York   b. Paris   c. New Orleans   d. Marseilles

60. In what year was the first movie to depict Santa Claus released?

a. 1896   b. 1903   c. 1922   d. 1930

answers

tots to teens puzzlers

Sugar Plums (1 point each)

1.	c	*Home Alone*
2.	a	Bernard
3.	b	That it was Christmas every day
4.	d	New York
5.	c	Prancer
6.	a	Scrooge McDuck
7.	c	Bob Cratchit
8.	c	Kermit the Frog

Candy Canes (2 points each)

9.	c	Macy's
10.	d	Arnold Schwarzenegger
11.	c	Gonzo
12.	c	The Bumpus's dogs
13.	c	A dog
14.	b	Jim Carrey

15.	c	A BB gun
16.	c	*Snow White*
17.	a	Get married
18.	b	Carface

Peanut Brittle (3 points each)

19.	c	*The Gift of the Magi*
20.	a	Angelique
21.	c	The toy will become frozen forever
22.	b	Blitzen
23.	d	Bert and Ernie
24.	d	Kevin
25.	d	Barney
26.	b	Edmund Gwenn
27.	b	A dog

Grown-ups' Brainteasers

Pumpkin Pies (1 point each)

28.	c	An angel gets its wings
29.	a	Sean Connery
30.	c	Jim Backus
31.	b	Judy Garland

32.	c	Rosemary Clooney
33.	d	343
34.	b	Richard Attenborough
35.	c	Dudley Moore
36.	b	The Martians
37.	a	Tim Burton
38.	b	He'll shoot his eye out

PLum Puddings (2 points each)

39.	b	*Holiday Inn* BONUS: 1942
40.	a	Donald O'Connor
41.	a	Albert Finney
42.	b	Natalie Wood
43.	c	Christopher Plummer
44.	c	*Meet Me in St. Louis*
45.	d	Fred Astaire
46.	a	Dan Aykroyd
47.	d	At a Chinese restaurant
48.	b	In someone else's home
49.	a	*It's a Wonderful Life*
50.	c	Michael Caine

Chestnuts (3 points each)

51. b   Hulk Hogan
52. c   Three
53. b & d   "Santa Claus is Coming to Town"; "Have Yourself a Merry Little Christmas" (Score 3 points for each correct answer; subtract 3 points for each incorrect answer.)
54. c   Angela Lansbury
55. b   *A Holiday Pageant at Home*
56. c   David Gallagher
57. a   *The Life of Brian*
58. d   Shirley Temple
59. d   Marseille
60. b   1903

CHRISTMAS ON THE TUBE

tots to teens puzzlers

Sugar Plums

1. In *A Charlie Brown Christmas,* what does Charlie Brown complain Christmas has become?
   - a. Too noisy
   - b. Too commercial
   - c. Too expensive
   - d. Too much work

2. In *Frosty the Snowman,* what are the first words Frosty says when he comes to life?
   - a. Merry Christmas
   - b. I'm alive!
   - c. Happy birthday
   - d. Where am I?

3. In *Rudolph the Red-Nosed Reindeer,* what is the name of the island where Rudolph and his friends find themselves?
   - a. Christmas Island
   - b. Island of Misfit Toys
   - c. Snow Island
   - d. Jamaica

4. What kind of meat does the Grinch carve at the end of *How the Grinch Stole Christmas*?
   - a. Who Hash
   - b. Turkey Dahoo Doray
   - c. Loosey Goosey
   - d. Roast Beast

5. In *A Charlie Brown Christmas,* what does Snoopy do that upsets Lucy?
   a. Steals her present
   b. Barks in her ear
   c. Licks her face
   d. Falls asleep during pageant rehearsal

6. In *Frosty the Snowman,* where does Frosty want to go to escape the rising temperature?
   a. Santa's workshop
   b. The North Pole
   c. The South Pole
   d. Florida
   BONUS: How does he want to travel?

7. Who brings Frosty back to life after he melts, in *Frosty the Snowman*?
   a. Santa Claus   b. Jack Frost   c. Pooh Bear   d. Mother Nature

8. At the end of *Frosty the Snowman,* how many times does the bad magician have to write, "I am very sorry for what I did to Frosty"?
   a. A hundred   b. A thousand   c. A million   d. A hundred zillion

9. In *Frosty Returns,* what is the name of the teacher?
   a. Miss Frump
   b. Miss Carbunkle
   c. Miss Toughnut
   d. Miss Nightshade

10. Who is chosen as king of the winter carnival in *Frosty Returns*?
    a. Frosty
    b. Santa
    c. Miss Carbunkle
    d. Professor Hinkle

Candy Canes

11. In *Rudolph the Red-Nosed Reindeer*, what is the name of the elf who would rather be a dentist?

    a. Marty   b. Hermey   c. Freddie   d. Bobbie

12. In *Eloise at Christmastime*, what is the name of Eloise's dog?

    a. Woofie   b. Weenie   c. Winston   d. Spot

13. In *How the Grinch Stole Christmas*, how many sizes too small is the Grinch's heart?

    a. Two   b. Three   c. Five   d. Ten

14. What is the name of the bad inventor in *Frosty Returns*?

    a. Professor Wizznut   c. Dr. Dormouse

    b. Mr. Twitchell   d. Professor Grimbit

15. What is the name of the villain who hates toys in the TV special *Santa Claus Is Coming to Town*?

    a. Burgermeister Meisterburger   c. Bah Humburger

    b. Burger the Terrible   d. Bugaboo Burger Bill

16. What is the first animal to appear in *Frosty the Snowman*?

    a. A rabbit   b. A horse   c. A cow   d. A duck

    BONUS: What is its name?

17. What is the name of the little girl who Frosty helps save in *Frosty the Snowman*?
    a. Katherine   b. Karen   c. Kimberley   d. Kendra
    BONUS: Who takes the little girl home?

18. In *Frosty Returns,* who ends up wearing the crown at the end of the program?
    a. The cat   b. Mr. Twitchell   c. Holly   d. Santa

19. In the *Garfield Christmas Special,* what present does Garfield give to Grandma Arbuckle?
    a. Old letters   c. Antique brooch
    b. New socks   d. Nothing: cats don't give presents!

20. In *A Flintstones Christmas Carol,* which character plays the part of Scrooge?
    a. Fred   b. Barney   c. Mr. Slate   d. Dino

PeaNut BRiTTLe

21. In *How the Grinch Stole Christmas,* what is the name of the mountain where the Grinch lives?
    a. Mount Nasty   c. Mount Crumpit
    b. Mount Who Pew   d. Mount Banana Peel

22. In *Frosty the Snowman,* what decoration is on the hat that is placed on Frosty's head?

    a. A flower   b. A flag   c. A sticker   d. A feather

23. In *Frosty the Snowman,* how much will Frosty's train ticket cost?

    a. $100.01   b. $3,000.04   c. $10,000.10   d. A zillion dollars

24. What is the name of the bad magician in *Frosty the Snowman*?

    a. Dr. Doolittle   c. Professor Hinkle

    b. Mr. Grumblewick   d. Marco the Magnificent

25. Whose hat brings Frosty to life in *Frosty Returns*?

    a. Mary Sunshine   c. Miss Carbunkle

    b. Holly DeCarlo   d. Hocus Pocus

26. In *Eloise at Christmastime,* what song does Eloise play on the piano in a duet with her friend Bill?

    a. "Jingle Bells"   c. "Winter Wonderland"

    b. "Sleigh Ride"   d. "Frosty the Snowman"

27. In *Frosty Returns,* what song do Frosty and the little girl sing together?

    a. "Frosty the Snowman"   c. "Winter Wonderland"

    b. "Sleigh Ride"   d. "Let There Be Snow"

28. What is the name of the invention that melts all the snow in *Frosty Returns*?
    a. Snow Away
    b. Snow-No-More
    c. Summer Wheeze
    d. Spring Breeze

29. What is the name of Holly's friend in *Frosty Returns*?
    a. Lucy   b. Bill   c. Patty   d. Charles

30. What is the real name of the Little Drummer Boy in the animated special by Arthur Rankin Jr. and Jules Bass?
    a. David   b. Jonathan   c. Aaron   d. Adam

GROWN-UPS' BRAINTEASERS

PUMPKIN PIES

31. Who sings the title song and narrates the original TV version of *Frosty the Snowman*?
    a. Bob Hope
    b. George Burns
    c. Donald O'Connor
    d. Jimmy Durante

32. Which hit reality show mounted a Christmas special in November 2003?
    a. *American Idol*
    b. *Fear Factor*
    c. *Survivor*
    d. *Joe Millionaire*

33. *The Man Who Saved Christmas* is based on the life of the inventor of what famous toy/game?
   a. Monopoly   b. Erector Set   c. Barbie   d. Parcheesi

34. Who stars in *The Christmas Shoes*?
   a. Rob Lowe   b. Billy Crystal   c. Brad Pitt   d. Jude Law

35. *The Homecoming—A Christmas Story* is a made-for-TV movie that has become a holiday season classic. What long-running series was it a pilot for?
   a. *The Beverly Hillbillies*   c. *The Andy Griffith Show*
   b. *The Waltons*   d. *Little House on the Prairie*

36. What insurance company created a TV commercial that featured Santa stuck in a chimney and a worried duck?
   a. John Hancock b. State Farm   c. Allstate   d. AFLAC

37. In *A Charlie Brown Christmas,* what is it that Lucy really wants for Christmas but never gets?
   a. A doll   b. A bike   c. A sled   d. Real estate

38. Which cartoon character asks, "Aren't we forgetting the true meaning of Christmas? You know, the birth of Santa?"
   a. Charlie Brown   c. Bart Simpson
   b. Bugs Bunny   d. Mickey Mouse

39. In *Frosty the Snowman,* how many reindeer are seen pulling Santa's sleigh?

a. Eight   b. Nine   c. Two   d. Four

40. Who plays Nanny in *Eloise at Christmastime*?

a. Angela Lansbury   c. Julie Andrews

b. Glenn Close   d. Mary Tyler Moore

BONUS: Name another film, now often seen on TV at Christmastime, in which the same star also plays a nanny.

Plum Puddings

41. In *A Charlie Brown Christmas,* which part is Shermie doomed to play every year in the Christmas pageant?

a. Joseph   b. A Wise Man   c. A shepherd   d. A sheep

42. Which singer plays the Scrooge character in *A Diva's Christmas Carol*?

a. Vanessa Williams   c. Whitney Houston

b. Diana Ross   d. Britney Spears

43. Which famous pianist wrote the music for *A Charlie Brown Christmas*?

a. Vince Guaraldi   c. David Foster

b. George Winston   d. Beethoven

44. In the television program *The O.C.*, what name does Seth give to the Christmas-Hanukkah season?

a. Chriskah   b. Chrismukkah   c. Hanmus   d. Hanuchris

45. In *A Very Brady Christmas,* Mrs. Brady plans on surprising her husband with a cruise to Greece at the same time he has planned a trip to which country?

a. France   b. Japan   c. Brazil   d. Australia

46. In what U.S. state is the made-for-television movie *Secret Santa* set?

a. Florida   b. Alaska   c. Indiana   d. New Mexico

47. Who was the only original Brady family kid not to appear in the TV movie *A Very Brady Christmas*?

a. Bobby (Mike Lookinland)   c. Jan (Eve Plumb)

b. Cindy (Susan Olsen)   d. Marsha (Maureen McCormick)

48. What is the name of the donkey in *Long-Eared Christmas Donkey*?

a. Nestor   b. Harry   c. Bartholomew   d. Eugene

49. Who plays the female lead in *The Homecoming—A Christmas Story*?

a. Sally Field   b. Patricia Neal   c. Sissy Spacek   d. Jessica Tandy

50. In *The Simpsons,* what Christmas-inspired name is given to the family's dog?

a. Jingle Bell   c. Plum Pudding

b. Rudolph   d. Santa's Little Helper

CHESTNUTS

51. On *Seinfeld,* what is the name of the holiday created to protest the commercialization of Christmas?
    a. Festivus
    b. Merryday
    c. Noëlmas
    d. Holiday-Shmoliday

52. Who narrates the original 1964 version of *Rudolph the Red-Nosed Reindeer*?
    a. Roy Rogers   b. John Wayne   c. Gene Autry   d. Burl Ives

53. Who stars in *Stealing Christmas*?
    a. Robin Williams
    b. Peter Falk
    c. Tony Danza
    d. Tom Cruise

54. What is the name of the small town where *Stealing Christmas* is set?
    a. Everwood   b. Evergreen   c. Eveready   d. Everton

55. Who was the lead animator for the original TV version of *How the Grinch Stole Christmas*?
    a. Walt Disney   b. Chuck Jones   c. Mel Blanc   d. Andy Warhol

56. Who supplies the voice of the magician in the original TV version of *Frosty the Snowman*?
    a. Jack Carson
    b. Billy DeWolfe
    c. Mel Blanc
    d. Jim Backus

57. Who supplies the voice of Frosty in *Frosty Returns*?
   a. John Belushi   c. John Goodman
   b. John Candy   d. John Wayne

58. What holiday classic story plays a central role in *Secret Santa*?
   a. *A Christmas Carol*   c. *The Little Match Girl*
   b. *The Gift of the Magi*   d. *A Visit from St. Nicholas*

59. Which actor, who for years starred as a detective in a popular TV series, plays a ubiquitous ghost in *Finding John Christmas*?
   a. James Garner   c. Robert Vaughn
   b. Peter Falk   d. Bill Cosby

60. In what year does the made-for-TV classic *The Homecoming—A Christmas Story* take place?
   a. 1929   b. 1933   c. 1939   d. 1942

answers

tots to teens puzzlers

Sugar Plums (1 point each)

1.	b	Too commercial
2.	c	Happy birthday
3.	b	Island of Misfit Toys
4.	d	Roast Beast
5.	c	Licks her face
6.	b	The North Pole BONUS: By train
7.	a	Santa Claus
8.	d	A hundred zillion
9.	b	Miss Carbunkle
10.	a	Frosty

Candy Canes (2 points each)

11.	b	Hermey
12.	b	Weenie
13.	a	Two

14.	b	Mr. Twitchell
15.	a	Burgermeister Meisterburger
16.	a	A rabbit BONUS: Hocus Pocus (Hocus will do)
17.	b	Karen BONUS: Santa Claus
18.	b	Mr. Twitchell
19.	a	Old letters
20.	a	Fred

Peanut Brittle (3 points each)

21.	c	Mount Crumpit
22.	a	A flower
23.	b	$3,000.04
24.	c	Professor Hinkle
25.	b	Holly DeCarlo
26.	c	"Winter Wonderland"
27.	d	"Let There Be Snow"
28.	c	Summer Wheeze
29.	d	Charles
30.	c	Aaron

Grown-ups' Brainteasers

Pumpkin Pies (1 point each)

31.	d	Jimmy Durante
32.	a	*American Idol*
33.	b	Erector Set
34.	a	Rob Lowe
35.	b	*The Waltons*
36.	d	AFLAC
37.	d	Real estate
38.	c	Bart Simpson
39.	d	Four
40.	c	Julie Andrews BONUS: *Mary Poppins*

Plum Puddings (2 points each)

41.	c	A shepherd
42.	a	Vanessa Williams
43.	a	Vince Guaraldi
44.	b	Chrismukkah
45.	b	Japan
46.	c	Indiana
47.	b	Cindy (Susan Olsen)
48.	a	Nestor

49. b Patricia Neal
50. d Santa's Little Helper

Chestnuts (3 points each)

51. a. Festivus
52. d Burl Ives
53. c Tony Danza
54. b Evergreen
55. b Chuck Jones
56. b Billy DeWolfe
57. c John Goodman
58. b *The Gift of the Magi*
59. b Peter Falk
60. b 1933

traditions
Old and New

tots to teens puzzlers

Sugar Plums

1. Which of these is not a part of the traditional North American Christmas dinner?
   a. Turkey
   b. Cranberry sauce
   c. Potatoes
   d. Horseradish

2. Which of these foods is not usually hung on a Christmas tree?
   a. Turkey
   b. Popcorn
   c. Candy canes
   d. Gingerbread cookies

3. At Christmastime, where is it traditional to kiss?
   a. Next to the tree
   b. At the front door
   c. In front of a snowman
   d. Under the mistletoe

4. Which of these flavours is not usually in Christmas sweets?
   a. Peppermint   b. Cinnamon   c. Ginger   d. Mustard

5. Which of these is not a traditional Christmas colour?
   a. Black   b. Green   c. Red   d. Gold

6. Which of these is a traditional Christmas flower?
   a. Pansy   b. Rose   c. Poinsettia   d. Dandelion

7. Which of these would you not find in your Christmas cracker?
   a. A funny hat   b. A joke   c. A prize   d. A puppy

8. What do we call the strands of shiny, metallic paper hung on the branches of Christmas trees?
   a. Wool   b. Spaghetti   c. Tinsel   d. Icing

9. What is a Christmas pageant?
   a. A beautiful red bird   c. A sugary dessert
   b. A play about the nativity   d. A holiday song

10. At Christmastime, which of these items is not usually used to wrap presents?
    a. Festive paper   c. Decorative bags
    b. Colourful ribbons   d. Saran Wrap

11. What kind of hat would you find inside a traditional Christmas cracker?
    a. A baby bonnet   c. A cowboy hat
    b. A wool cap   d. A paper crown

Candy Canes

12. What fruit is used to make a Christmas pomander ball?
    a. Apple   b. Pear   c. Orange   d. Tangerine

13. According to tradition, what should you do to a plum pudding before serving it?
    a. Sing to it
    b. Dance around it
    c. Throw it at the Christmas tree
    d. Light it on fire

14. In which country did shortbread, a traditional Christmas dessert, originate?
    a. Mexico   b. Jamaica   c. Germany   d. Scotland

15. What country is generally credited with popularizing the Christmas tree?
    a. England   b. Scotland   c. Germany   d. Sweden

16. What Christmas dessert is made from almonds, egg whites, and sugar?
    a. Gingerbread   b. Marzipan   c. Candy canes   d. Shortbread

17. Which of these items is not an ingredient in traditional Christmas eggnog?
    a. Milk   b. Eggs   c. Spices   d. Chocolate

18. Which of these is not usually found in a Christmas fruitcake?
    a. Green cherries   b. Nuts   c. Raisins   d. Strawberries

Peanut Brittle

19. Which of these is not traditionally found in an Advent calendar?
    a. Candy   b. Pictures   c. Mistletoe   d. Toys

20. The pope's annual Christmas greeting is usually delivered from where?
    a. Nativity Square   c. St. Paul's Cathedral
    b. St. Peter's Square   d. St. Mark's Square

21. According to tradition, what food should you eat on each of the twelve days of Christmas to ensure good luck for the coming year?
    a. Candy canes   b. Gum drops   c. Mincemeat pies   d. Turkey

22. Which famous Victorian author has had a strong influence on our modern-day Christmas traditions?
    a. Thomas Hardy   c. Emily Brontë
    b. Charles Dickens   d. Lewis Carroll

23. In nineteenth-century London, what kind of ethnic dessert inspired the invention of the Christmas cracker?
    a. Mexican wedding cake   c. French madeleines
    b. Chinese fortune cookies   d. Greek baklava

24. If you are making a snowflake ornament for your Christmas tree, how many sides should it have to be realistic?
    a. Four   b. Six   c. Eight   d. Ten

25. Which spice is used to make a Christmas pomander ball?
    a. Cinnamon   b. Cloves   c. Mint   d. Nutmeg

26. Christmas seals are special stamps that have been sold for many years to raise funds for what area of medicine?
    a. Heart disease   c. Kidney disease
    b. Lung disease   d. Cancer

Grown-ups' Brainteasers

Pumpkin Pies

27. Who is generally credited with inventing the Christmas card?
    a. Charles Dickens   c. Sir Henry Cole
    b. Prince Albert   d. Ebenezer Scrooge

28. Whom did the angel at the top of the tree originally represent?
    a. The Virgin Mary   c. The Christ Child
    b. The angel Gabriel   d. God

29. According to tradition, it is important to add three spices to a mince pie to represent the gifts of the Magi. What are the three spices?
    a. Cinnamon, cloves, and nutmeg   c. Thyme, pepper, and oregano
    b. Basil, sage, and garlic   d. Ginger, salt, and marjoram

30. What is the traditional Scottish name for the New Year's celebration?
    a. Robbie Burns Day   c. Haggis
    b. Hogmanay   d. Candlemas

31. The tradition of the Christmas tree is believed to have been brought to the United States by what group of people?
    a. The Dutch settlers of Manhattan Island
    b. Hessian soldiers fighting with the British in the Revolutionary War
    c. The Pilgrims
    d. The settlers of the Jamestown colony

32. What inspired the name "Boxing Day"?
    a. Fights among holiday revellers
    b. Church alms boxes
    c. Ceremonial burning of empty Christmas boxes
    d. A dance performed at Christmastime in England

33. What is the favourite activity of Canadians on Boxing Day?
    a. Sleeping   b. Skiing   c. Shopping   d. Skating

34. In which country did the tradition of the Christmas cracker originate?
    a. England   b. France   c. Germany   d. United States

35. The tradition of kissing under the mistletoe was started by what people?
    a. Celts   c. Germanic tribes
    b. Romans   d. Medieval Christians

PLum Puddings

36. How long is the yule log supposed to burn?
    a. Until Christmas morning   c. Until Boxing Day
    b. Until New Year's Day   d. For the twelve days of Christmas

37. Who is credited with popularizing the tradition of setting up a nativity scene at Christmas?
    a. Queen Victoria   c. St. Francis of Assisi
    b. Pope Clement II   d. Martin Luther

38. A bowl of walnuts has been part of many mid-winter celebrations since Roman times. What do they represent?
    a. Prosperity   b. Good health   c. Fertility   d. Fame

39. College football games have become a holiday tradition in the United States. Where was the first New Year's Day bowl game played?
   a. Miami, Florida
   c. Pasadena, California
   b. New Orleans, Louisiana
   d. Houston, Texas

40. How many Masses are traditionally celebrated by Roman Catholics on Christmas Day?
   a. One
   b. Two
   c. Three
   d. Four

41. Guy Lombardo and his Royal Canadians were a New Year's Eve tradition for many years at which New York City hotel?
   a. The Plaza
   c. The Commodore
   b. The Waldorf-Astoria
   d. The Algonquin

42. When did the Roman Catholic custom of celebrating midnight Mass on Christmas Eve begin?
   a. First century
   c. Eighth century
   b. Fifth century
   d. Tenth century

43. Although the Christmas pudding has been around for centuries, when did the version that we eat now first become popular?
   a. During Elizabethan times
   c. In the eighteenth century
   b. During Victorian times
   d. In the early twentieth century

44. When did the tradition of sending Christmas cards begin?
   a. 1900
   b. 1840
   c. 1750
   d. 1920

45. What country was the first to popularize Christmas cards?
     a. United States   b. Germany   c. Great Britain   d. Australia

Chestnuts

46. The Christmas wreath is said to be derived from an old Roman custom of giving evergreen branches to mark the New Year. What did the branches signify?
     a. Rebirth   b. Good health   c. Long life   d. Fertility

47. Which ancient peoples are the creators of what became the modern Christmas plum pudding?
     a. The Celts   b. The Romans   c. The Saxons   d. The Vikings

48. Who is credited with inventing the Christmas cracker?
     a. Benjamin Franklin   c. Tom Smith
     b. Charles Dickens   d. Marcel Ouimet

49. In what year did the Christmas cracker make its debut?
     a. 1775   b. 1836   c. 1870   d. 1901

50. Who does the word "yuletide" come from?
     a. The Vikings   c. The Celts
     b. The Romans   d. The Germanic tribes

51. What Stone Age ritual is believed to be the forerunner of Christmas gift-giving?
    a. Farmers' food exchanges   c. Family presents to newborns
    b. Hunters' sacrifices to gods   d. Bridal dowries

52. An obscure urban legend recommends hiding a peculiar kind of Christmas ornament in your Christmas tree for good luck. What is the ornament?
    a. A pebble   c. A spool of thread
    b. A glass pickle   d. A ham sandwich

53. In the Franche Comté region of France, gifts were, according to legend, delivered by a half-witch, half-fairy called Tante Arie. How did she travel?
    a. In a sleigh   c. On a broomstick
    b. Riding a donkey   d. Flying, using her wings

54. It has become a tradition for the British monarch to broadcast a Christmas message. Which one was the first to do so?
    a. Edward VII   b. George V   c. George VI   d. Elizabeth II
    BONUS: What year did the broadcast take place?

55. In which country do people eat their traditional Christmas Eve meal at a table covered by a linen cloth under which straw has been strewn, to represent the manger?
    a. Ukraine   b. Poland   c. Hungary   d. Austria

56. Who is credited with having introduced the tradition of the Christmas tree?
   a. St. Francis of Assisi   c. St. Nicholas
   b. St. Boniface   d. St. Valentine

57. Where did the glass Christmas tree ball originate?
   a. England   b. Venice   c. Bohemia   d. Hungary

58. Many countries now issue special Christmas postage stamps. Which country did it first?
   a. France   b. United States   c. Great Britain   d. Canada

59. We often write "Xmas" as an abbreviation for Christmas. What does the "X" stand for?
   a. The cross
   b. The first Greek letter in Christos (Christ)
   c. An underground symbol for Christianity from Roman times
   d. Nothing

60. The Rose Bowl football game has become a New Year's tradition in the United States. But what event was substituted for football in the Rose Bowl for several years?
   a. Baseball   c. Track and field
   b. Horse racing   d. Chariot racing

answers

tots to teens puzzLers

SugaR pLums (1 point each)

1.	d	Horseradish
2.	a	Turkey
3.	d	Under the mistletoe
4.	d	Mustard
5.	a	Black
6.	c	Poinsettia
7.	d	A puppy
8.	c	Tinsel
9.	b	A play about the nativity
10.	d	Saran Wrap
11.	d	A paper crown

CaNDy CaNes (2 points each)

12.	c	Orange
13.	d	Light it on fire
14.	d	Scotland
15.	c	Germany
16.	b	Marzipan
17.	d	Chocolate
18.	d	Strawberries

PeaNut BRittLe (3 points each)

19.	c	Mistletoe
20.	b	St. Peter's Square
21.	c	Mincemeat pies
22.	b	Charles Dickens
23.	b	Chinese fortune cookies
24.	b	Six
25.	b	Cloves
26.	b	Lung disease

Grown-ups' Brainteasers

Pumpkin Pies (1 point each)

27.	c	Sir Henry Cole
28.	c	The Christ Child
29.	a	Cinnamon, cloves, and nutmeg
30.	b	Hogmanay
31.	b	Hessian soldiers fighting with the British in the Revolutionary War
32.	b	Church alms boxes
33.	c	Shopping
34.	a	England
35.	d	Medieval Christians

Plum Puddings (2 points each)

36.	d	For the twelve days of Christmas
37.	c	St. Francis of Assisi
38.	a	Prosperity
39.	c	Pasadena, California
40.	c	Three
41.	b	The Waldorf-Astoria
42.	b	Fifth century
43.	b	During Victorian times

| 44. | b | 1840 |
| 45. | c | Great Britain |

Chestnuts (3 points each)

46.	b	Good health
47.	a	The Celts
48.	c	Tom Smith
49.	c	1870
50.	a	The Vikings
51.	a	Farmers' food exchanges
52.	b	A glass pickle
53.	b	Riding a donkey
54.	b	George V BONUS: 1932
55.	b	Poland
56.	b	St. Boniface
57.	c	Bohemia
58.	d	Canada
59.	b	The first Greek letter in Christos (Christ)
60.	d	Chariot racing

CHRISTMAS PRESENT

The title of this chapter may have left you wondering. Does it refer to the presents that await us under the tree on Christmas morning? Or is it about how we celebrate (or don't celebrate) Christmas in the twenty-first century?

The answer is: both. And that adds a fun twist to the questions that follow. You can't be sure whether you're going to be asked about a popular gift or have your brain tested by a query about a recent Christmas-related event or modern-day tradition. So be alert!

tots to teens puzzlers

Sugar Plums

1. What are you supposed to do when you see people standing under a sprig of mistletoe?
   a. Kiss them
   b. Shake hands with them
   c. Give them a present
   d. Step on their feet

2. Which of these is not usually a rule in a secret Santa gift exchange?
   a. Not telling whom the gift is from
   b. Spending only a certain amount of money
   c. Wrapping the present
   d. Dressing up like elves

3. What present do naughty little children find in their stockings on Christmas morning?

    a. An onion   c. A stinky diaper

    b. A lump of coal   d. Nothing

4. Where is the most common place to hang a Christmas wreath?

    a. On the front door   c. On top of the Christmas tree

    b. On your head   d. By the chimney with care

5. What kind of bird is the most popular to serve for Christmas dinner?

    a. Chicken   b. Goose   c. Duck   d. Turkey

6. When you decorate a Christmas tree, what is the first thing usually put on?

    a. Tinsel   c. Balls

    b. Lights   d. Star or angel on the top

7. What is another way to say "decorating the tree"?

    a. Dressing the tree   c. Trimming the tree

    b. Painting the tree   d. Clothing the tree

8. How does Santa get into our home on Christmas Eve?

    a. He knocks on the door

    b. He comes through the window

    c. He slides down the chimney

    d. He digs a tunnel up through the floor

9. When you build a snowman, which of these items would you probably not use?

    a. Snow   b. A carrot   c. A top hat   d. A bathing suit

Candy Canes

10. Which U.S. city is famous for its Christmastime department store window displays?

    a. Boston   b. Chicago   c. New York   d. Philadelphia

11. According to superstition, what happens to people who don't eat any plum pudding at Christmastime?

    a. They go to bed hungry
    b. They'll lose a friend in the new year
    c. Santa will take back their gifts
    d. The Plum Pudding Ghost will haunt them forever

12. What is the name of the African-American holiday celebration that takes place between December 26 and January 1 every year?

    a. Botswana   b. Festivus   c. Kwanzaa   d. Hanukkah

13. Despite different fads, which toy consistently sells the most every Christmas?

    a. Barbie   b. Lego   c. Blocks   d. Monopoly

14. What is the name of the ballet performed every Christmas?
    a. *Swan Lake*
    c. *Romeo and Juliet*
    b. *The Nutcracker*
    d. *Santa's Elves*

15. What is a popular way of counting down the days to Christmas?
    a. Using a calendar filled with chocolate
    b. Lighting a candle for twelve days
    c. Putting up a new decoration every day
    d. Eating a special dinner for ten days

16. In the television special *Frosty Returns,* what does Frosty wear besides a hat?
    a. Gloves
    c. A bow tie
    b. Shoes
    d. A sweater
    BONUS: What colour is it?

17. What internet publication bills itself as "Santa's Official Newsletter"?
    a. *The Santa Review*
    c. *The Christmas Tribune*
    b. *The North Pole Times*
    d. *The Sleigh Ride Express*

18. Which decoration can be dangerous on a Christmas tree?
    a. Garlands   b. Candles   c. Icicles   d. Candy canes

Peanut Brittle

19. Where did the world-famous toy store FAO Schwartz open its first store?
    a. London   b. Paris   c. New York   d. Toronto

20. Where does New York City's official Christmas tree stand?
    a. Times Square   c. Rockefeller Center
    b. Central Park   d. Fifth Avenue

21. Which Native Canadian people might be found dining on whale, caribou, and seal for Christmas dinner?
    a. The Inuit   b. The Cree   c. The Haida   d. The Iroquois

22. In England, the Christmas pantomime has been popular for three centuries. What is it?
    a. A silent re-creation of the nativity story
    b. A school play by children
    c. A comical theatrical presentation, often with a fairy-tale theme
    d. A street show in which participants exchange funny pants

23. What space probe failed to phone home after it landed on Mars on Christmas Day 2003?
    a. *Spirit*   b. *Beagle 2*   c. *Rover*   d. *Odyssey*

24. What is the name of the Pokémon Christmas CD released in 2001?
    - a. *Christmas Fun*
    - b. *Christmas Spirit*
    - c. *Christmas Party*
    - d. *Christmas Bash*

25. Who brings gifts to children in South America on Christmas Eve?
    - a. Santa Claus
    - b. The Three Kings
    - c. Baby Jesus
    - d. The Virgin Mary

GROWN-UPS' BRAINTEASERS

PUMPKIN PIES

26. The paper hats in Christmas crackers are usually shaped like crowns. Why?
    - a. In tribute to the British monarchy
    - b. As a modern symbol of the king and queen of the old Twelfth Night celebrations
    - c. Because the original Christmas crackers contained tiny crown-shaped tokens
    - d. To remind everyone of Christ the King

27. Which area under U.S. administration is the first to enjoy Christmas Day each year?
    - a. Virgin Islands
    - b. Puerto Rico
    - c. Hawaii
    - d. Guam

28. Which of these countries does not celebrate Boxing Day?
    a. Canada   b. United States   c. England   d. Australia

29. According to Miss Manners, which of the following is not an
    acceptable way of handling an unwanted Christmas present?
    a. Exchanging it for something else
    b. Donating it to charity
    c. Selling it at a yard sale
    d. Asking the giver to take it back and try again

30. The author of what bestselling Christmas book used some of the
    profits to establish a shelter for abused children in Salt Lake City,
    Utah?
    a. *Skipping Christmas*   c. *The Christmas Shoes*
    b. *The Christmas Box*   d. *The Christmas Train*

31. Which of these items is not mentioned in an 1881 *Harper's
    Bazaar* article entitled "Christmas Presents for Men"?
    a. Paperweights   b. Inkstands   c. Ties   d. Tobacco boxes

32. Which famous bowl game was not played on New Year's Day in
    2002 for the first time in eighty-six years?
    a. Sugar Bowl   b. Orange Bowl c. Rose Bowl   d. Cotton Bowl

33. Advent, the period for preparing to celebrate Christ's birth,
    begins on the Sunday closest to the feast day of which saint?
    a. Peter   b. Mark   c. Paul   d. Andrew

34. Why do we make lots of noise at midnight on New Year's Eve?
    a. Because we've had too much to drink
    b. To ward off evil spirits
    c. To celebrate the departure of the old year
    d. To rid ourselves of all worries

35. What is the zodiac sign of a baby born on Christmas Day?
    a. Scorpio   b. Sagittarius   c. Capricorn   d. Aquarius

36. In which decade might you have found yourself in the middle of a riot if trying to buy a Cabbage Patch Doll for a Christmas present?
    a. 1960s   b. 1970s   c. 1980s   d. 1990s

37. Which world-famous toy store filed for bankruptcy protection for a second time just before Christmas 2003?
    a. Toys "R" Us   b. FAO Schwarz   c. Hamleys   d. Disney Store

Plum Puddings

38. America's official national Christmas tree, the General Grant Tree, is located in what state?
    a. New York   c. South Carolina
    b. Washington   d. California
    BONUS: What kind of tree is it?

39. In what country were Santa's elves laid off in 2003 at a Christmas theme park attraction in the Arctic because of poor attendance?

a. Canada   b. Russia   c. Norway   d. Finland

40. In what year did Barbie make her debut under the Christmas tree?

a. 1955   b. 1959   c. 1964   d. 1970

41. What year did Monopoly first become a popular present for Christmas?

a. 1925   b. 1935   c. 1945   d. 1955

42. "Hello, Boys! Make Lots of Toys!" was the holiday advertising catchphrase for which popular construction toy?

a. Lego   b. Erector Set   c. Mega Bloks   d. Tinkertoys

43. In 1963, the department store Neiman Marcus offered what "supergift" in its annual holiday catalogue for the cost of $18,700?

a. A submarine built for two   c. A Christmas tree made of gold
b. A reindeer team and sled   d. A diamond-encrusted Santa hat

44. In what country in 2003 did labour unions demand that stores limit the playing of Christmas carols to one hour a day, calling their constant playing "psychological terrorism"?

a. Great Britain   b. Russia   c. Austria   d. Turkey

45. According to an 1881 *Harper's Bazaar* article entitled "Christmas Presents for Men," what was the cost of a "Christmas hymnal bound in black monkey-skin, with silver monogram or gilt initials and fit to size for the waistcoat pocket"?
   a. $1   b. $5   c. $10   d. $20

46. In which year might you have found a Pet Rock waiting for you under the Christmas tree?
   a. 1915   b. 1935   c. 1955   d. 1975

47. What country's prime minister rejected a move to release all children being detained by the Immigration Department, just before Christmas 2003?
   a. Canada   b. Great Britain   c. Australia   d. New Zealand

48. How long was the Church of the Nativity in Bethlehem held under siege in 2002?
   a. Nineteen days   c. Thirty-nine days
   b. Twenty-nine days   d. Forty-nine days

Chestnuts

49. Which overwhelmingly Muslim country declared in 2002 that the date of Christmas celebrations by their Christian minority would henceforth be a national holiday?
   a. Turkey   b. Jordan   c. Egypt   d. Malaysia

50. Which year was Tickle Me Elmo the must-have toy for Christmas?
     a. 1996   b. 1997   c. 1998   d. 1999

51. What town banned the sale of Santa Claus items from its market
    in 2003?
     a. St. Ives, England   c. St. Moritz, Switzerland
     b. St. Wolfgang, Austria   d. St. Tropez, France

52. In what North American city in 2000 did a protest group
    vandalize merchants who put up Christmas decorations before
    December 1?
     a. Mexico City   b. New Orleans   c. Montreal   d. New York

53. What game was one of the most popular Christmas gifts in 1900?
     a. Parcheesi   b. Ping-Pong   c. Scrabble   d. Tiddlywinks

54. What is the ritual lighting of a brandy-soaked plum pudding
    meant to symbolize?
     a. The guiding light   c. The hope of the world
     b. The heat of the sun   d. The warmth of the hearth

55. If you find a thimble in your slice of plum pudding, what does it
    signify, according to ancient lore?
     a. A good homemaker   c. Imminent marriage
     b. A saintly life   d. Great wealth

56. Since the sixth century, Candlemas was the day that marked the end of the Christmas season in many countries. It has since become what modern-day observance?
    a. Boxing Day   c. New Year's Day
    b. New Year's Eve   d. Groundhog Day

57. In what country was it illegal right up to the 1990s to travel to church on Christmas Day by any means other than walking?
    a. Ireland   b. Germany   c. Great Britain   d. France

58. Every year on December 23 in Oaxaca, Mexico, there is a grand festival marked by the carving of ornate vegetable sculptures. What is it known as?
    a. Night of the Radishes   c. Afternoon of the Avocado
    b. Eve of the Eggplant   d. Occasion of the Onion

59. Erector Set was the most popular Christmas gift in the early twentieth century. Who invented it?
    a. A.C. Gilbert   c. Alexander Graham Bell
    b. Thomas Edison   d. Eli Whitney

60. What is the maximum possible number of days in Advent, the period for preparing to celebrate Christ's birth?
    a. Twelve   b. Sixteen   c. Twenty-eight   d. Thirty
    BONUS: What is the minimum number of days?

answers

tots to teens puzzlers

Sugar Plums (1 point each)

1.	a	Kiss them
2.	d	Dressing up like elves
3.	b	A lump of coal
4.	a	On the front door
5.	d	Turkey
6.	b	Lights
7.	c	Trimming the tree
8.	c	He slides down the chimney
9.	d	A bathing suit

Candy Canes (2 points each)

10.	c	New York
11.	b	They'll lose a friend in the New Year
12.	c	Kwanzaa

13.	b	Lego
14.	b	*The Nutcracker*
15.	a	Using a calendar filled with chocolate
16.	c	A bow tie BONUS: Red with white polka dots ("Red" will do)
17.	b	*The North Pole Times* (www.northpoletimes.com)
18.	b	Candles

Peanut Brittle (3 points each)

19.	c	New York
20.	c	Rockefeller Center
21.	a	The Inuit
22.	c	A comical theatrical presentation, often with a fairy-tale theme
23.	b	*Beagle 2*
24.	d	*Christmas Bash*
25.	c	Baby Jesus (Niño Jesús)

Grown-ups' Brainteasers

Pumpkin Pies (1 point each)

26.	b	As a modern symbol of the king and queen of the old Twelfth Night celebrations
27.	d	Guam
28.	b	United States
29.	d	Asking the giver to take it back and try again
30.	b	*The Christmas Box*
31.	c	Ties
32.	c	Rose Bowl
33.	d	Andrew
34.	b	To ward off evil spirits
35.	c	Capricorn
36.	c	1980s
37.	b	FAO Schwarz

Plum Puddings (2 points each)

38.	d	California BONUS: A sequoia
39.	d	Finland
40.	b	1959
41.	b	1935
42.	b	Erector Set

43.	a	A submarine built for two
44.	c	Austria
45.	c	$10
46.	d	1975
47.	c	Australia
48.	c	Thirty-nine days

Chestnuts (3 points each)

49.	c	Egypt
50.	a	1996
51.	b	St. Wolfgang, Austria
52.	c	Montreal
53.	b	Ping-Pong
54.	b	The heat of the sun
55.	b	A saintly life
56.	d	Groundhog Day
57.	c	Great Britain
58.	a	Night of the Radishes
59.	a	A.C. Gilbert
60.	c	Twenty-eight BONUS: Twenty-one

Olde tyme
Christmas

tots to teens Puzzlers

Sugar Plums

1. Which of these might be found in a Christmas pie in the Middle Ages?
   a. Blackbirds   b. Ox tongues   c. Pigeons   d. All three

2. According to legend, what will happen to you if you refuse a piece of mince pie?
   a. Sickness   b. Bad luck   c. Punishment   d. A kiss

3. What unusual pairing of foods is found in the old-fashioned version of a mince pie?
   a. Shrimp and cheese   c. Nuts and eggs
   b. Meat and fruit   d. Tuna and Cheerios

4. Which of these was not one of the toy instruments a child might have received for Christmas in 1881?
   a. Tambourine   b. Lute   c. Mandolin   d. Synthesizer

5. Back in the 1600s, the shape of Christmas candy canes was inspired by which item from the nativity story?
   a. A manger   c. Straw
   b. A donkey   d. A shepherd's crook

6. What was the most popular bird served for dinner in Christmases past?

   a. Turkey   b. Pheasant   c. Duck   d. Goose

7. If you lived a hundred years ago, what would your Christmas gift definitely *not* have been made of?

   a. Plastic   b. Wood   c. Straw   d. Paper

CaNDy CaNes

8. Which of these was not a traditional Christmas treetop decoration in the nineteenth century?

   a. A flag   c. A star
   b. An angel   d. A red Santa Claus hat

9. Which of these was the featured dessert at Christmas dinner in the nineteenth century?

   a. Plum pudding   c. Prune pudding
   b. Raisin pudding   d. Banana pudding

10. An old-fashioned Christmas parlour game in Victorian England was known as *Hunt the …?*

    a. Turkey   b. Thimble   c. Toy train   c. Ninja turtle

11. How old is the poem "A Visit from St. Nicholas"?
    a. Less than 25 years   c. More than 100 years
    b. Less than 50 years   d. More than 150 years

12. The winter solstice was marked in ancient times by a celebration from which we get many of our modern-day Christmas traditions. What do we know the winter solstice as today?
    a. Halloween   c. New Year's Day
    b. First day of winter   d. Christmas Eve

13. The concept of Santa Claus was originally brought to North America by Dutch colonists. What famous island did they first settle?
    a. Greenland   b. Iceland   c. Manhattan   d. Hawaii

14. Who conducted the first Christmas Eve midnight Mass?
    a. St. Peter   c. The king of Judea
    b. The pope   d. John the Baptist

Peanut Brittle

15. For a time, Christmas pies were shaped like what?
    a. A log   b. A shoe   c. A boat   d. A crib

16. The yule log was first symbolized in a holiday treat called *bûche de Noël*. Where did it originate?
    a. Germany   b. Spain   c. France   d. Italy

17. What is a *bûche de Noël*?
    a. Bread pudding   c. Mince pie
    b. Chocolate cake   d. Apple crumble

18. Until the seventeenth century, what was one of the most common dishes in Britain at Christmastime?
    a. Blackbird pie   b. Mistletoe pie   c. Cranberry pie   d. Humble pie

19. A novelty Christmas present for little girls in 1881 was an eating-doll. A bit of candy put in her mouth would come out where?
    a. Ear   b. Hand   c. Belly button   d. Foot

20. Which of these ingredients is not included in a traditional Victorian recipe for plum pudding?
    a. Eggs   b. Sugar   c. Bread   d. Plums

21. What was the object of the Victorian Christmas game Snap Dragon?
    a. To snatch currants out of a bowl of flaming brandy
    b. To stuff as many peanuts into your mouth as possible
    c. To find a toy dragon hidden somewhere in the house
    d. To stand on your head longer than anyone else

22. At the end of the nineteenth century, the first artificial Christmas tree was created in Germany out of what material?
   a. Plastic   b. Feathers   c. Aluminum foil   d. Camel hair

23. According to one ancient legend, at midnight on Christmas Eve all hibernating bees wake up and start humming in unison. What do they hum?
   a. "Hallelujah Chorus"   c. "100th Psalm"
   b. Lord's Prayer   d. "Ode to Joy"

24. Complete this sentence found in a 1901 article about Christmas tree ornaments from *The Delineator* magazine: "One of the quickest made festoons for a Christmas tree, and one which has never been thought of until now, is decorations of …"
   a. Paper   b. Plastic   c. Styrofoam   d. Tinfoil

25. Which famous cartoon character did the novelty band the Royal Guardsmen write a Christmas song about in the 1960s?
   a. Snoopy   c. Mickey Mouse
   b. Bugs Bunny   d. Beetle Bailey

26. In what country were electric lights first used to replace candles on Christmas trees?
   a. Germany   b. United States   c. England   d. Canada

27. Which of these was not eaten for Christmas dinner in medieval England?

    a. Goose   b. Turkey   c. Swan   d. Peacock

28. In 1995, the tenth anniversary collection of a popular comic strip became one of the Christmas season's bestselling books just weeks after the cartoonist announced his retirement. What was the comic strip?

    a. *Peanuts*   c. *Calvin and Hobbes*
    b. *Blondie*   d. *Doonesbury*

Grown-ups' Brainteasers

Pumpkin Pies

29. Which British monarch discarded the swan in favour of turkey for the royal Christmas dinner?

    a. King George III   c. Queen Victoria
    b. Queen Anne   d. William of Orange

30. Which of these names was applied to Christmas during the time Oliver Cromwell governed as Lord Protector in Britain?

    a. Satan's Working Day   c. Papists' Massing Day
    b. Heathens' Feasting Day   d. All three

31. The largest Christmas cracker on record was 181 feet 11 inches long. Where was it made?
   a. Germany   b. Great Britain   c. Australia   d. Canada

32. What war was halted by an undeclared truce on Christmas Day?
   a. American Civil War   c. First World War
   b. Revolutionary War   d. Second World War

33. Which of the following was not born on Christmas Day?
   a. Humphrey Bogart   c. Sir Isaac Newton
   b. Rod Serling   d. Jesus Christ

34. Which did Elvis Presley say was his favourite Christmas song?
   a. "White Christmas"
   b. "Blue Christmas"
   c. "Ring Christmas Bells"
   d. "Rockin' Around the Christmas Tree"

35. What fruit was usually added to wassail bowls in England in olden times?
   a. Plums   b. Peaches   c. Apples   d. Figs

36. Who officially abolished Christmas in England while he ruled there?
   a. Julius Caesar   c. Oliver Cromwell
   b. William the Conqueror   d. George III

37. The creator of Rudolph the Red-Nosed Reindeer was working for what company at the time?
    a. Wal-Mart
    b. Montgomery Ward
    c. Macy's
    d. Sears Roebuck

Plum Puddings

38. On what day of the year was the yule log brought into the home in medieval times?
    a. December 6   b. December 24   c. December 25   d. January 1

39. What was often done to a yule log when it was brought to the fireplace? (There are two correct answers.)
    a. Everyone touched it
    b. A blessing was said for it
    c. Wine was poured over it
    d. It was given a name

40. Candles were originally used on Christmas trees to symbolize who or what?
    a. Return of the sun
    b. Jesus Christ
    c. The Virgin Mary
    d. Peace on Earth

41. Christmas pies were made illegal in England in which century?
    a. Twelfth   b. Fifteenth   c. Seventeenth   d. Nineteenth

42. What were ashes from a yule log used for? (There are two correct answers.)
   a. To ward off evil spirits   c. To preserve meat
   b. To cure illnesses   d. To make mulled wine

43. In eighteenth-century Germany, how many candles were considered to be appropriate for a twelve-foot-tall tree?
   a. Fifty   b. One hundred   c. Two hundred   d. Four hundred

44. Who banned Twelfth Night celebrations in Britain?
   a. Oliver Cromwell   c. Queen Elizabeth I
   b. Henry VIII   d. Queen Victoria

45. Which historical figure called mistletoe, holly, and ivy "ungodly branches of superstition"?
   a. Napoleon   c. Oliver Cromwell
   b. Queen Victoria   d. Gandhi

46. In olden times, what was the first Monday after Epiphany called?
   a. Sad Monday   c. Plough Monday
   b. Blue Monday   d. Market Monday

47. A 1901 article about Christmas tree ornaments from *The Delineator* magazine suggests fashioning an edible chimney sweep ornament out of what kind of food?
   a. Marshmallows   c. Gingerbread
   b. Prunes   d. Mashed potatoes

48. When did the Salvation Army start sending out people dressed as Santa Claus to raise money for the poor at Christmas?

    a. 1850s   b. 1890s   c. 1920s   d. 1940s

Chestnuts

49. In which century A.D. was December 25 decreed by the Church to be the day on which Christ's birthday would be celebrated?

    a. Second   b. Ninth   c. Fourth   d. Eleventh

50. Who was the first British royal to erect a Christmas tree?

    a. King Henry VIII   c. Prince William of Orange
    b. Queen Elizabeth I   d. Queen Charlotte

51. What benefit was supposed to come to those who dragged home a yule log?

    a. Long life   b. Good luck   c. Great wealth   d. Many children

52. What was used to light a yule log?

    a. A red-hot poker
    b. Straw from an old broom
    c. A piece of wood from last year's yule log
    d. A torch made from twigs taken from the log itself

53. The discovery of what in a slice of Twelfth Night cake allowed the lucky finder to become king of the revels?
    a. A ring   b. A thimble   c. A bean   d. A plum

54. A charm depicting what was considered a symbol of good luck in early Christmas crackers?
    a. A thimble   b. A black cat   c. A fir tree   d. A horseshoe

55. When were electric lights first used on Christmas trees?
    a. 1882   b. 1896   c. 1902   d. 1910

56. Where was the first midnight Mass held?
    a. St. Peter's Square   c. Nativity Square
    b. St. Paul's Cathedral   d. Church of St. Mary Major

57. In old England, what name was given to the drink made for the wassail bowl?
    a. Sheep dip   c. Warmgetting
    b. Lambswool   d. Cow juice

58. When were the first Christmas cards put on sale?
    a. 1792   b. 1814   c. 1843   d. 1890

59. What was it about the first Christmas card that outraged many Victorians?
   a. No mention was made of Jesus
   b. Children were depicted holding glasses of wine
   c. The card did not contain the word "Christmas"
   d. The family shown on the card was poor

60. In Victorian England, what was a Goose Club?
   a. Women who wore silly hats at Christmas
   b. A gaggle of geese that was being fattened for Christmas dinner
   c. An organization to which low-paid workers contributed money in the hope of winning a Christmas goose
   d. A London club that served roast goose at Christmastime

61. A law passed in Great Britain in 1551 banned all sports on Christmas Day except one. Which one?
   a. Fox hunting   b. Shooting   c. Fishing   d. Archery

62. How did Good King Wenceslas die?
   a. He drowned
   b. He was thrown by his horse
   c. He was murdered
   d. He was hit by an arrow during battle

answers

tots to teens puzzlers

Sugar Plums (1 point each)

1.	d	All three
2.	b	Bad luck
3.	b	Meat and fruit
4.	d	Synthesizer
5.	d	A shepherd's crook
6.	d	Goose
7.	a	Plastic

Candy Canes (2 points each)

8.	d	A red Santa Claus hat
9.	a	Plum pudding
10.	b	Thimble
11.	d	More than 150 years
12.	b	First day of winter
13.	c	Manhattan
14.	b	The pope

Peanut Brittle (3 points each)

15.	d	A crib
16.	c	France
17.	b	Chocolate cake
18.	d	Humble pie
19.	d	Foot
20.	d	Plums
21.	d	To snatch currants out of a bowl of flaming brandy
22.	b	Feathers
23.	c	"100th Psalm"
24.	d	Tinfoil
25.	a	Snoopy
26.	b	United States
27.	b	Turkey
28.	c	*Calvin and Hobbes*

Grown-ups' Brainteasers

Pumpkin Pies (1 point each)

29.	c	Queen Victoria
30.	d	All three
31.	c	Australia
32.	c	First World War
33.	d	Jesus Christ
34.	b	"Blue Christmas"
35.	c	Apples
36.	c	Oliver Cromwell
37.	b	Montgomery Ward

Plum Puddings (2 points each)

38.	b	December 24
39.	b & c	A blessing was said for it; Wine was poured over it (Score 2 points for each correct answer; subtract 2 points for each incorrect answer.)
40.	b	Jesus Christ (as the Light of the World)
41.	c	Seventeenth
42.	a & b	To ward off evil spirits; To cure illnesses (Score 2 points for each correct answer; subtract 2 points for each incorrect answer.)

43.	d	Four hundred
44.	d	Queen Victoria
45.	c	Oliver Cromwell
46.	c	Plough Monday
47.	b	Prunes
48.	b	1890s

CHESTNUTS (3 POINTS EACH)

49.	c	Fourth
50.	d	Queen Charlotte
51.	b	Good luck
52.	c	A piece of wood from last year's yule log
53.	c	A bean
54.	b	A black cat
55.	a	1882
56.	d	Church of St. Mary Major
57.	b	Lambswool
58.	c	1843
59.	b	Children were depicted holding glasses of wine
60.	c	An organization to which low-paid workers contributed money in the hope of winning a Christmas goose
61.	d	Archery
62.	c	He was murdered

the
Nativity Story

tots to teens Puzzlers

Sugar Plums

1. What were the shepherds doing when the angel appeared to tell them about the birth of Jesus?
   - a. Having dinner
   - b. Milking their goats
   - c. Watching their flocks
   - d. Praying

2. Who gave the first gifts to Baby Jesus?
   - a. The Three Wise Men
   - b. St. Nicholas
   - c. Shepherds
   - d. Angels

3. What did the Three Wise Men use to guide them to the Christ Child?
   - a. A map
   - b. Street signs
   - c. A star
   - d. A large arrow

4. Who were the first people other than Mary and Joseph to see Baby Jesus?
   - a. The Three Wise Men
   - b. Shepherds
   - c. Apostles
   - d. Soldiers

5. Which of these animals does not usually appear in scenes of the stable where Jesus was born?
   - a. Ox
   - b. Sheep
   - c. Donkey
   - d. Pig

6. In which town was Jesus born?
   a. Jerusalem   b. Bethlehem   c. Judea   d. Jericho

7. What was the name of Mary's husband?
   a. Jeremiah   b. John   c. Joseph   d. James

8. According to the Bible, at what time of day was Jesus born?
   a. Morning   c. Afternoon
   b. Lunchtime   d. Night

9. What do we celebrate on December 25?
   a. Getting presents   c. Eating turkey
   b. No school   d. The birth of Jesus

Candy Canes

10. What was Joseph's job?
    a. Carpenter   b. Bricklayer   c. Stonemason   d. TV repair man

11. Bethlehem was a part of what great empire?
    a. Egyptian   b. Ottoman   c. Roman   d. Greek

12. In which direction did the Three Wise Men travel in their search
    for Baby Jesus, according to St. Matthew?
    a. North   b. South   c. East   d. West

13. In the nativity story, how did Mary dress Baby Jesus after he was born?
    a. In pyjamas
    b. In Pampers
    c. In a nightgown
    d. In swaddling clothes

14. Scientists have tried to explain the mysterious Star of Bethlehem. Which of these do they *not* suggest it was?
    a. A meteor   b. A supernova   c. A comet   d. An airplane

15. What is a nativity scene called in French?
    a. *Gâteau*   b. *Manteau*   c. *Bateau*   d. *Crèche*

16. Which of these was not a gift to Baby Jesus from the Three Wise Men?
    a. Myrrh   b. Silver   c. Gold   d. Frankincense

17. Joseph and Mary travelled to Bethlehem from which city?
    a. Nazareth   b. Jerusalem   c. Cairo   d. Jericho

18. Why did Joseph and Mary travel to Bethlehem?
    a. To be taxed
    b. To visit family
    c. Because Joseph had work there
    d. To take a vacation

19. On which animal did Mary ride into Bethlehem?
    a. Horse   b. Camel   c. Donkey   d. Goat

20. What is the real birthday of Jesus?
    a. December 25
    b. January 1
    c. January 6
    d. No one knows for sure

PeaNut BRittLe

21. When the angel of the Lord appeared to the shepherds, what was their first reaction?
    a. Joy   b. Fear   c. Curiosity   d. Awe

22. Bethlehem was also known as the city of whom?
    a. John   b. David   c. Abraham   d. Solomon

23. The Wise Men are also known as what? (There are two correct answers. You must get both to score points.)
    a. Rabbis   b. Magi   c. Apostles   d. Kings

24. Who was the king of Judea when Jesus was born?
    a. Caesar Augustus
    b. Herod
    c. Solomon
    d. David

25. What animals are said to have been in the stalls on either side of Baby Jesus?
    a. Sheep and lamb
    b. Goat and pig
    c. Ox and horse
    d. Donkey and cow

26. After Jesus was born, what did the angel of the Lord tell Joseph?
   a. To follow his star
   b. That the king would destroy the child
   c. That he should go back to Jerusalem
   d. That the Wise Men would guard the baby

27. Where is the Church of the Nativity?
   a. Rome   b. Bethlehem   c. Jerusalem   d. New York

28. If you went to Bethlehem today, where would you be?
   a. Israel   b. Jordan   c. Egypt   d. West Bank

Grown-ups' Brainteasers

Pumpkin Pies

29. How did King Herod feel when he heard of the birth of Jesus?
   a. Elated   b. Humbled   c. Troubled   d. Reverent

30. In what biblical country was Bethlehem located?
   a. Egypt   b. Judea   c. Persia   d. Greece

31. Which of these gospels contains the nativity story that is most often quoted at Christmas?
   a. St. Matthew   b. St. Mark   c. St. Luke   d. St. John

32. What is the name of the outdoor public place in Bethlehem where crowds often gather to celebrate Christmas?
   a. Gethsemane
   b. Manger Square
   c. Christ's Square
   d. Stable Square

33. How long did the Three Wise Men search for Baby Jesus?
   a. Three days
   b. Twelve days
   c. A fortnight
   d. One year

34. Which Christmas Eve tradition is based on the belief that Baby Jesus was born precisely at the stroke of twelve?
   a. Candlemas
   b. Midnight Mass
   c. Michaelmas
   d. Santa's arrival

35. What was King Herod's reaction when the Wise Men did not return from their visit to Baby Jesus to tell him where the child could be found?
   a. He set out to find the child himself
   b. He ordered that all the children in Bethlehem under the age of two be killed
   c. He sent his own delegates to give the child gifts on his behalf
   d. He ordered that all the newborn babes in the kingdom be brought to him

Plum Puddings

36. Joseph was said to be from the house of whom?
    a. Jacob   b. David   c. Abraham   d. Zechariah

37. Only one of the gospels tells the story of the Three Wise Men. Which one is it?
    a. St. Matthew   b. St. Mark   c. St. Luke   d. St. John

38. Name a gospel that does not refer to the nativity story at all. (There are two correct answers. Score 2 points for each correct answer; subtract 2 points for each incorrect answer.)
    a. St. Matthew   b. St. Mark   c. St. Luke   d. St. John

39. When Mary and Joseph left Bethlehem with Baby Jesus, where did they go?
    a. Jerusalem   b. Nazareth   c. Egypt   d. Galilee

40. What is myrrh?
    a. A gemstone   b. A spice   c. A fruit   d. A perfume

41. Which Christian faith believes that Jesus was born at midnight?
    a. Baptist   c. Lutheran
    b. Presbyterian   d. Roman Catholic

42. According to the story as told in St. Matthew, how many Wise Men came to pay homage to the Christ Child?
    a. Two
    b. Three
    c. Five
    d. No number given

43. According to tradition, which of these was not one of the Wise Men?
    a. Gaspar   b. Melchior   c. Porthos   d. Balthasar
    BONUS: Which famous threesome did the odd man out belong to?

44. According to Chapter One of St. Matthew, upon learning of Mary's pregnancy, how does Joseph feel?
    a. Overjoyed   b. Angry   c. Confused   d. Awestruck

45. According to modern-day versions of the Bible, what does Joseph first consider doing when he learns that Mary is going to have a baby?
    a. Say a prayer
    b. Divorce her quietly
    c. Ask God for guidance
    d. Speak to her parents

Chestnuts

46. What was myrrh commonly used for in Biblical times?
    a. Food preservation
    b. Flavouring
    c. Sun protection
    d. Embalming

47. According to the Bible, who was the angel that appeared to Mary to foretell of the birth of Jesus?

a. Michael   b. Gabriel   c. Zacharias   d. Ezekiel

48. In Spain, one animal from the nativity story holds a special place for Christians because they believe it breathed on Baby Jesus and kept him warm. Which is the animal?

a. Donkey   b. Cow   c. Goat   d. Ox

49. According to St. Matthew, the angel of the Lord appeared to Joseph to tell him that the child Mary was carrying had been conceived by the Holy Ghost. What was Joseph doing at the time?

a. Walking in a field   c. Sleeping
b. Working at his trade   d. Praying

50. Which pope officially established December 25 as Christ's birthday?

a. Pius II   b. Julius I   c. Gregory V   d. John Paul I

51. Which Roman emperor made Christmas a holiday?

a. Augustus   b. Claudius   c. Justinian   d. Theodosius

52. How was John's mother, Elizabeth, related to Jesus' mother, Mary?

a. They were cousins   c. They were twins
b. They were half sisters   d. They were not related

53. Which Roman emperor made Herod king of the Jews?
    a. Julius Caesar   b. Octavian   c. Tiberius   d. Nero

54. In what year did Herod become king?
    a. 40 B.C.   b. 27 B.C.   c. 35 B.C.   d. 50 B.C.

55. In St. Matthew, how many generations are said to have elapsed between each of the following events: from Abraham to David; from David until the "carrying away" of Babylon; and from the fall of Babylon to the birth of Jesus?
    a. Seven   b. Ten   c. Fourteen   d. Sixteen

56. The feast of the Epiphany on January 6 celebrates the arrival of the Wise Men. But in the Eastern Orthodox Church, it has a different symbolism. What is it?
    a. The day of Jesus' birth by the Greek calendar
    b. The day of Jesus' baptism
    c. The day of Mary's immaculate conception
    d. The day Joseph and Mary fled from King Herod

57. According to St. Luke, what event took place eight days after Jesus was born?
    a. Baptism   c. An angelic visitation
    b. Circumcision   d. The flight into Egypt

58. Where does St. Luke say Joseph and Mary took Jesus after leaving Bethlehem?

    a. Nazareth   b. Egypt   c. Jerusalem   d. Sinai

59. St. Luke speaks of a sacrifice being offered to the Lord by Joseph and Mary after Jesus' birth. What was the sacrifice?

    a. A goat   c. A pair of turtle doves
    b. A lamb   d. A chicken

60. According to St. Matthew, how long did Joseph, Mary, and Jesus remain in Egypt?

    a. Fifty days   c. Until Jesus was a grown man
    b. One year   d. Until the death of King Herod

answers

tots to teens puzzlers

Sugar Plums (1 point each)

1.	c	Watching their flocks
2.	a	The Three Wise Men
3.	c	A star
4.	b	Shepherds
5.	d	Pig
6.	b	Bethlehem
7.	c	Joseph
8.	d	Night
9.	d	The birth of Jesus

Candy Canes (2 points each)

10.	a	Carpenter
11.	c	Roman
12.	c	East
13.	d	In swaddling clothes
14.	d	An airplane

15.	d	*Crèche*
16.	b	Silver
17.	a	Nazareth
18.	a	To be taxed
19.	c	Donkey
20.	d	No one knows for sure

Peanut Brittle (3 points each)

21.	b	Fear
22.	b	David
23.	b & d	Magi; Kings
24.	b	Herod
25.	c	Ox and horse
26.	b	That the king would destroy the child
27.	b	Bethlehem
28.	d	West Bank

Grown-ups' Brainteasers

Pumpkin Pies (1 point each)

29.	c	Troubled
30.	b	Judea
31.	c	St. Luke
32.	b	Manger Square
33.	b	Twelve days
34.	b	Midnight Mass
35.	b	He ordered that all the children in Bethlehem under the age of two be killed

Plum Puddings (2 points each)

36.	b	David
37.	a	St. Matthew
38.	b & d	St. Mark; St. John (Score 2 points for each correct answer; subtract 2 points for each incorrect answer.)
39.	c	Egypt
40.	b	A spice
41.	d	Roman Catholic
42.	d	No number given
43.	c	Porthos BONUS: The Three Musketeers

| 44. | c | Confused |
| 45. | b | Divorce her quietly |

Chestnuts (3 points each)

46.	d	Embalming
47.	b	Gabriel
48.	b	Cow
49.	c	Sleeping (the angel appeared to him in a dream)
50.	b	Julius I
51.	c	Justinian
52.	a	They were cousins
53.	b	Octavian
54.	a	40 B.C.
55.	c	Fourteen
56.	b	The day of Jesus' baptism
57.	b	Circumcision
58.	c	Jerusalem
59.	c	A pair of turtle doves
60.	d	Until the death of King Herod

send us your christmas trivia questions

Despite all the research we've done, you may still have some unanswered Christmas questions of your own. Or you may think of a question to which you already know the answer that you would like to share with others. In either case, send it to us. If you don't know the answer, we'll do our best to find it and include it in the next edition of *Quizmas*. If you do know the correct response, give it to us and save us some work. Mail it to the address below or visit our website at www.quizmas.net and use the special email form there. We'd be delighted to hear from you

Quizmas
Suite 181
16715 – 12 Yonge Street
Newmarket, Ontario
Canada   L3X 1X4
www.quizmas.net

Bibliography

Books

Bowler, Gerry. *The World Encyclopedia of Christmas.* Toronto: McClelland and Stewart, 2000.

Collins, Ace. *Stories Behind the Best-Loved Songs of Christmas.* Grand Rapids, MI: Zondervan, 2001.

Comfort, David. *Just Say Nöel.* New York: Simon and Schuster, 1995.

Count, Earl W., and Alice Lawson Count. *4000 Years of Christmas: A Gift from the Ages.* Berkeley, CA: Ulysses Press, 1997.

Daniel, Mark, ed. *A Golden Christmas Treasury.* London: Macmillan, 1991.

De Sike, Yvonne. *Christmas.* N.P.: Hachette Illustrated, 2003.

Dickens, Charles. *Christmas Books, Volume 2.* Harmondsworth, England: Penguin Books, 1971.

———. *The Posthumous Papers of the Pickwick Club.* London: J.M. Dent and Sons, 1907.

Editors of *The New Yorker. Christmas at The New Yorker.* New York: Random House, 2003.

Federer, William J. *There Really Is a Santa Claus: The History of Saint Nicholas & Christmas Holiday Traditions.* St. Louis: Amerisearch, 2002.

Foster, Anne H., and Ann Grierson. *High Days and Holidays in Canada*. Toronto: Ryerson Press, 1970.

Hague, Michael. *Michael Hague's Family Christmas Treasury*. New York: Henry Holt, 1995.

Holy Bible, New International Version. Grand Rapids, MI: Zondervan, 1989.

Holy Bible, King James Version. Grand Rapids, MI: Zondervan, 2002.

Isherwood, Shirley. *Miracles, Whales and Wonderful Tales: Voices from the Bible*. New York: Random House, 2002.

Keyes, Nelson Beecher. *Reader's Digest Story of the Bible World*. Pleasantville, NY: Reader's Digest Association, 1962.

Maier, Paul L. *In the Fullness of Time*. Grand Rapids, MI: Kregel Publications, 1997.

Matthews, John. *The Winter Solstice*. Wheaton, IL: Theosophical, 1998.

Moore, Clement C. *The Night Before Christmas*. Racine, WI: Western Publishing, 1975.

Morris, Desmond. *Christmas Watching*. London: Jonathan Cape, 1992.

Nissenbaum, Stephen. *The Battle for Christmas*. New York: Alfred A. Knopf, 1996.

Nobbman, Dale V. *Christmas Music Companion Fact Book*. Anaheim Hills, CA: Centerstream, 2000.

Peters, Edward. *Europe and the Middle Ages*. 3rd ed. Upper Saddle River, NJ: Prentice Hall, 1997.

Restad, Penne L. *Christmas in America*. New York: Oxford University Press, 1995.

Rouse, Judy M. *History, Legends & Folklore of Christmas*. Lincoln, NE: iUniverse, 2001.

Segall, Barbara. *The Christmas Tree*. New York: Clarkson N. Potter, 1995.

————. *The Holly and the Ivy*. New York: Clarkson N. Potter, 1991.

Studwell, William. *The Christmas Carol Reader*. New York: Haworth Press, 1995.

Tabori, Lena, ed. *The Little Big Book of Christmas*. New York: William Morrow, 1999.

Wagenknecht, Edward, ed. *The Fireside Book of Christmas Stories*. New York: Grosset and Dunlap, 1945.

World Book Encyclopedia. Chicago: World Book-Childcraft International, 1978.

Periodicals and Wire Services

Associated Press

Bloomberg News

Globe and Mail. Toronto, ON: Bell Globemedia Publishing.

News-Press. Fort Myers, FL: Multimedia Holdings Corp.

People. New York: Time Inc.

Toronto Star. Toronto, ON: Torstar Corp.

USA Today. McLean, VA: Gannett Co.

Websites

Amazon.ca <www.amazon.ca>

Amazon.com <www.amazon.com>

Catholic Encyclopedia <www.newadvent.org/cathen>

Christmas <www.christmas.com>

Christmas Archives <www.christmasarchives.com>

Christmas in Canada <members.tripod.com/~MitchellBrown/christmas/
joytotheworld.html>

Christmas Inventions <www.inventors.about.com/library/inventors/
blchristmas.htm>

Christmas Literature <www.jeannepasero.com/xmaslit.html>

Christmas Parlour Games <www.netguides.org.uk/guides/
christmasparlourgames.html>

Christmas Quiz <www.brownielocks.com/quiz.html>

Christmas Song Lyrics <christmas-song-lyrics.com>

Christmas Traditions in France and Canada
<www.culture.gouv.fr/culture/noel/angl/noel.htm>

Daley, Michael J. "Nativity: A Story You Can Get Into," *Youth Update*
<www.americancatholic.org/Newsletters/YU/ay1100.asp>

Dickens and Christmas <www.fidnet.com/%7Edap1955/dickens/
christmas.html>

East Central University <www.ecok.edu>

Encarta Encyclopedia <encarta.msn.com>

Family Games—Christmas Trivia
     <www.familygames.com/features/quizzes/xmasquiz.html>

Global Christmas <www.expatica.com/source/site_article.asp?subchannel_id=24
     &story_id=3222>

Graham Newnham's Web Pages <www.pathefilm.freeserve.co.uk/xmas.htm>

Guy Lombardo Wing <www.dotydocs.com/lombardo.htm>

How Christmas Works <www.people.howstuffworks.com/christmas.htm>

Hymns and Carols of Christmas <www.hymnsandcarolsofchristmas.com>

National Christmas Tree Association <www.realchristmastrees.org>

Netguides <www.netguides.org.uk/guides/Christmas.html>

North Pole Times <www.northpoletimes.com>

Santa Facts <www.northpole.com/Clubhouse/Q&A/Santa.html>

Santa's Christmas Around the World <www.santaclaus.com/world.html>

Santa's Net <www.santas.net/aroundtheworld.htm>

Teachers First Victorian Christmas <www.teachersfirst.com/lessons/
     vic-xmas.htm>

Victorian Christmas <www.victoriana.com/christmas>

Victorian Christmas Scrap Album <www.scrapalbum.com/vxhome.htm>

Whychristmas.com <www.whychristmas.com>